Boston's Freedom Trail

Trace the Path of American History

NINTH EDITION

Cindi D. Pietrzyk

travel

Guilford, Connecticut

All the information in this guidebook is subject to change. We recommend that you call ahead to obtain current information before traveling.

Editor: Kevin Sirois
Project Editor: Meredith Dias
Layout: Kirsten Livingston
Text design: Sheryl P. Kober
Map: Daniel Lloyd © Rowman & Littlefield

Original text by Robert Booth

ISSN 1559-1808
ISBN 978-0-7627-7298-8

Distributed by NATIONAL BOOK NETWORK

To my husband Stephen,
I'm so glad you chose to walk the long path with me.

Contents

About the Author

Cindi D. Pietrzyk is a freelance writer and editor based in Connecticut. She has been writing and working in the publishing industry for sixteen years, both in-house and as a freelancer. She started her career as a journalist and worked for a year covering the beat before moving on to book publishing.

In 1998 she started Pietrzyk Publishing and in that capacity has worked as project manager, copy editor, proofreader, and writer. In addition to *Boston's Freedom Trail*, she has also contributed to *Short Nature Walks: Connecticut* (Globe Pequot Press) and served as editor of the 19th edition of *The Connecticut Walk Book: East*, published by the Connecticut Forest and Park Association. She is also co-owner of Coastal Editing (www.coastalediting.com), a web-based editorial services company.

Acknowledgments

So many people helped out with this edition of the book to make sure I had all the facts straight. Input from those who helped was invaluable. I thank each and every one of you for taking the time to review text and get back to me with changes, suggestions, and additions. Special thanks goes to Kristin Bezio and Theresa Cooney at King's Chapel; Patrick M. Leehey at the Paul Revere House; Bob Damon at Old North Church; Laura O'Neill, Margherita M. Desy, and Sarah Watkins at the USS *Constitution* Museum for all their input and help.

I simply can't thank Ethan Beeler of the National Park Service enough for fielding all of my e-mails and questions and taking the time to review seemingly endless text.

Also, my gratitude goes to Sam Jones for taking the time to read through the book, offer his opinions, point out common misconceptions, and not be afraid to tell me when I was just plain wrong. Your input was vital and set all the wheels in motion.

I can't forget my editor at Globe Pequot Press, Kevin Sirois, who never got tired of my need for clarification and whose vision for the book kept me on track. Thank you, too, to project editor Meredith Dias, the one who kept us all to the timeline and made sure it all came together.

Finally, to my family who trekked into the city with me and spent hours on the Trail—you are the best. To my daughters, Charley, Samantha, and Kailey—thank you for putting up with all my hours at the computer and understanding when the laundry wasn't done and dinner wasn't ready.

Lastly, I would like to acknowledge all those volunteers and employees who work tirelessly along the Trail to keep history alive and preserve the past for upcoming generations. May you all never forget how important you are.

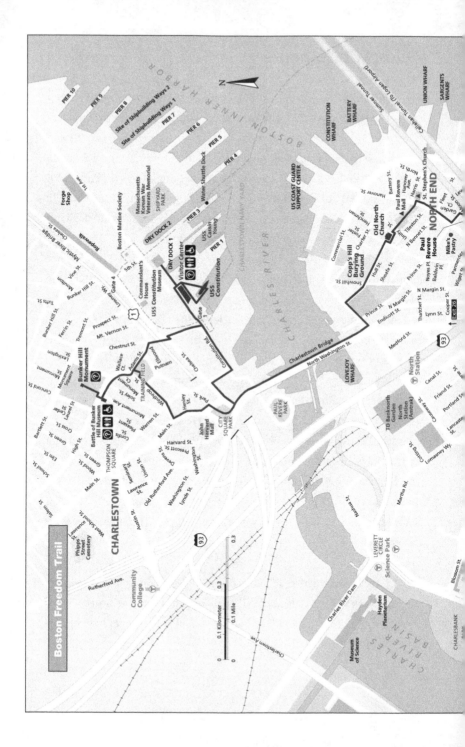

Boston Freedom Trail

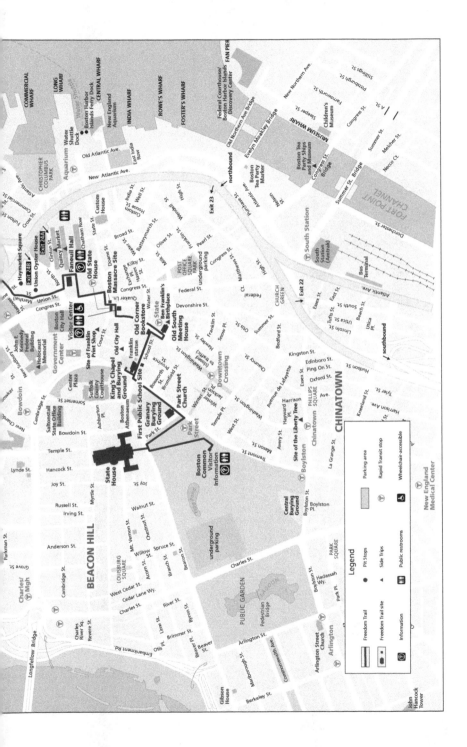

VISITOR INFORMATION

For many years the Freedom Trail in Boston was a concept without a name. In 1950 a Boston newspaperman, William G. Schofield, came to the realization that the greatest number of sites sacred to the beginnings of our republic anywhere in the United States were located in Boston, and moreover they were all within easy walking distance of one another. He decided something should be done to somehow mark a pathway to each site. His actions, with some help from others, resulted in what is now known as the Freedom Trail. For a complete history on how it happened, be sure to visit the Freedom Trail Foundation's website at www.thefreedomtrail.org.

Today, the Freedom Trail is one of the most popular walking tours in America. It covers 2.5 miles and is easy to follow if you pay attention. The path is marked by painted red lines or red bricks set into the pavement, and there are also signs along the way. You'll have to be on the

PHOTO BY STEPHEN W. PIETRZYK

lookout for the next site as you follow along. This book includes a chapter on each of the official sites, as well as sidebars on influential and colorful players of the time. This new edition also includes suggested **Side Trips** to nearby historic attractions that don't stray too far from the red line, as well as **Pit Stops,** points of interest where you might want to take a break from the proceedings and shop or grab a bite to eat.

Many of the sites along the Trail are free and allow you to stop, visit, and explore, while the three museums along the Trail—the Old South Meeting House, the Old State House, and the Paul Revere House—all charge admission. A discounted, combined admission to the Old South Meeting House and Paul Revere House is available in the form of a Patriots' Pass, which can be purchased online at www.paulreverehouse .org/trail or http://store.thefreedomtrail.org/freedomtrailitems.aspx but can also be purchased at the Old South Meeting House. If your trip is in less than two weeks, it is recommended that you purchase the tickets once you hit town as opposed to online.

Brave the Cold

Don't assume that the Freedom Trail can only be enjoyed in the warm weather. Winter is an excellent time to see the sights—without the crowds. Keep in mind, though, that the frequency of tours is reduced to once daily from December through March, and they leave from the Common only.

Seven of the sites along the Trail fall inside the Boston National Historic Park and are well staffed by Park Service Rangers. These sites include Old South Meeting House, the Old State House, Faneuil Hall, the Paul Revere House, Old North Church, USS *Constitution* (not the museum, though), and Bunker Monument and Museum. The National Park Service plays a large part in preserving these sites.

Wear Comfortable Shoes

Bear in mind that the Freedom Trail is a walking tour; do not attempt to drive it. Much of the Trail meanders through the twisting and curved, sometimes cobblestoned, streets that are the original paths and byways established by the first colonists, and many parts of the Trail are not accessible by car. The best way to see everything is to walk, but keep in mind that the Trail is not a loop. While you can start anywhere along the Trail, you will not eventually end up where you started unless you backtrack. If you don't wish to retrace your steps, either park a car at both ends, grab the ferry across the harbor, jump on the T, or navigate a shortcut back to your parking spot. The most convenient and logical starting points and parking areas are under Boston Common or near USS *Constitution* in Charlestown; however, there are lots of other choices in between.

Many people complete the entire walk in one day, but just as many say they wish they had split it into two days to lessen the amount of walking, especially if you want to stop and explore the buildings or stop for a bite to eat at the numerous restaurants along the Trail. History, after all, wasn't made in just one day!

Tours

The **Freedom Trail Foundation** offers a variety of tours for those who don't wish to go it alone. These tours are conducted by period-costumed guides who will not only transport you to all the sites but also back in history. You can choose one (or more) tours based on your area or areas of interest. During the peak season (Apr through Nov), these tours leave from a variety of starting points, depending on their focus. In the off-season (Dec through Mar), there is one daily tour at 12 p.m. that departs from the Visitor Center on the Common, however, it is subject to weather-related cancellation, so it's best to call ahead to be sure it's still on. There is a charge for these tours. For more information or to buy tickets, visit www.thefreedomtrail.org and click on "walking tours."

If you decide to forego a guided tour, consider downloading one of the multiple apps available online, or purchase the Foundation's audio file that can be downloaded as an MP3 file for your own player or played on an audio player available at the Visitor Center on the Common. These offer some great info on the places you'll see, and you can even listen to it on the way to Boston so you can be ready for what you're about to discover. (You'll need Internet access, however, to listen.)

Handicapped Accessibility

While the Foundation strives to keep as much as possible of the Trail wheelchair-accessible, some sites are not due to the age of the building and historical preservation restrictions. Also, the Trail has numerous hills and some long stretches between sites. We have indicated which sites included in the book have partial or complete accessibility and the best ways to find it, but we highly recommend that you call ahead before your travels to get details for your specific needs.

The **National Park Service** also offers tours along the Trail, and those are free. These 90-minute tours are offered weather permitting and depart from the Boston National Historical Park Visitor Center (located behind the Old State House, 15 State St.). Because reservations are not accepted (except for groups of 10 or more) and tours can fill up quickly (each is limited to 30 people), you'll want to arrive a good half hour before the scheduled tour time to receive a sticker from the Park ranger, which will ensure your spot on the tour. Tours start at 2 p.m. on weekdays, and 10 a.m. and 2 p.m. on weekends from mid- to late Apr through mid- to late June, and Sept 1 through

Nov. From June 21 through Aug 31, tours run daily at 10 a.m., 2 and 3 p.m. For more information call (617) 242-5642 or visit www.nps.gov/bost/planyourvisit/guidedtours.htm.

If you prefer to ride, there are trolley tours, but these are unofficial and may not take you to all the sites along the Trail. For information on these tours, visit www.trolleytours.com/boston/freedom-trail.asp.

Getting There

If you plan on driving into Boston, you're going to have to find a place to park, which can be expensive. You have choices, though. If you have planned on starting your tour of the Trail at the Commons, then the logical choice is the Boston Common Garage, located under Boston Common. (Cool, huh?) Weekday rates here range from $8 (for an hour; you'll need more to explore the Trail) to $27 (for twenty-four hours, you won't need that long!). But, weekend rates are cheaper at $11 per day. Entrance to the Boston Common Garage is from Charles Street, which heads north (one-way) between the Common and the Public Garden. Look for the red, white, and blue Boston Common sign with a big P on it. Once you "pahhk your cahh," take the elevator up

---

So Close

You know those signs you see on the highway telling you how close to Boston you are? They actually measure the distance to the dome on the State House, not the distance to the city limits.

---

to the ground level and head to one of the four handicapped-accessible kiosks that provide otherwise invisible pedestrian access to the garage. You should find yourself on the Charles Street/Beacon Street corner of the Common. Be sure to note which kiosk you emerged from so you will know how to return and find your car! The garage is open from 7 a.m. to 7 p.m. on weekdays and from 7 a.m. to 3 p.m. Sat and Sun. For more information, including driving directions, visit www.mccahome .com/bcg.html or call (617) 954-2098 or (617) 954-2096 (automated).

If you'd rather start your trek from the north end of the Trail, you could consider parking in the **Charlestown Navy Yard** near USS *Constitution*, where there are a limited number of parking spaces available. If you don't luck out with one of those, and you most likely will not find on-street parking, you can check out other commercial parking garages in the area. A good website for information on these is www.boston-discovery-guide .com/boston-parking-garages-near-north-end.html.

If you weren't lucky enough to get close to the Trail, don't worry. Boston is equipped with an efficient public transportation system. Buses operate along the route of the Freedom Trail about every 10 to 15 minutes, 7 days a week, generally from 6 a.m. to midnight. The **Massachusetts Bay Transportation Authority's (MBTA)** website provides information about which station is nearest to each of the sites as well as schedules, routes, and fares. Information is also available by calling (800) 392-6100.

Bus fare ranges from $1.25 to $1.50 for adults; children 11 and younger ride free with an adult. Subway fare runs from $1.70 to $2 per person. Many stations and the information booth on Boston Common display free subway maps. Visitor passes, which cost $9 per person for one day and $15 per person for 7 days, give you unlimited rides. It's easy, and there's usually someone there to give you a hand in figuring out what you need and where you want to go.

The CharlieCard can be purchased at Back Bay Station and at Downtown Crossing Station on non-holiday weekdays from 8:30 a.m. to 5 p.m. There are a variety of programs for seniors, handicapped, and student riders. For more information call (617) 222-5976, (617) 222-5854 (TTY), or (800) 543-8287 or visit www.mbta.com.

The MBTA strives to have all their buses and stations wheelchair accessible, in fact their website claims that they hope to become the "global benchmark" for accessible public transportation. For more information visit www.mbta.com/riding_the_t/accessible_services/default .asp?id=16901, or call the numbers listed earlier.

That should be everything you need to know to have a successful trip. If you bring this book along, you'll get a good dose of the local history that you'll be seeing along the Trail and gain some insight into what life was like "back then." Good luck and happy history hunting!

Boston Common

Bounded by Park, Tremont, Boylston, Charles, and Beacon Streets

There's nothing common about **Boston Common,** America's oldest public park. Set on more than 44 acres south of the Charles River and west of Boston Harbor, the Common is the southern point of the Freedom Trail.

The Common itself has seen more than 377 years of history since it was purchased by Puritan settlers and its land set aside for such important public uses as pasturage for goats and cows and for public punishment and executions.

The Common's central location made it the focal point of the town. Often the place for public meetings, punishments, and celebrations, if it was happening, it was probably happening on the Common. The Puritans especially seem to have a preference for humiliation and ridicule as a means of enforcing their unyielding laws as evidenced in their public punishments. For thievery, those caught could be branded, or whipped if caught twice. For a third offense the punishment was death by hanging in the public gallows.

Some of the unfortunate citizens who met their punishment on the Common included **William Robinson, Marmaduke Stevenson, William Leddra,** and **Mary Dyer,** who were convicted of being Quakers and launched into eternity by hanging. Those of Quaker belief were not welcome in Massachusetts and were banished from the colony. If they chose to return, the penalty was death by hanging. The Quakers were peaceful people who believed that divine revelation came from within, not from ordained leaders. They taught that worship was through silent prayer, not preaching. They did not believe in music or art. They did not believe in war.

Mary Dyer was a woman of such faith. Born in 1611, Dyer was an English Puritan who eventually came to embrace the Quaker faith. She supported **Anne Hutchinson** (see sidebar in the **Old Corner Bookstore** chapter on p. 43), and together they defied Puritan law and organized Bible study groups to further their idea that one didn't need to consult a clergyman to hear God, but that God spoke directly to an individual and he or she only had to listen. In the late 1630s, Dyer left along with Hutchinson who had been banished from the colony. Settling in Rhode Island, she traveled with her husband to England, where she first heard Quaker founder George Fox speak. So moved was she by the ideology that she herself became a Quaker preacher. Remaining in England until the late 1650s, Dyer then returned to Boston to pro-

---

One of Boston's Firsts

Rev. William Blackstone already lived on the slope of Beacon Hill when the Puritans arrived in Boston. Having remained in the New World after the failed Gorges expedition, The Reverend was enjoying his solitude with his many books for company. Once his new neighbors settled, however, Reverend Blackstone, tired of having so much company and, not being tolerant of the unyielding Puritan view of life, withheld 6 acres at the top of the hill and sold the rest of his homestead to the town in 1634. Blackstone resettled about 35 miles away on a hill overlooking what is today the Blackstone River. He later went on to become good friends with **Roger Williams** and regularly spoke at his church in Providence, Rhode Island. Blackstone died in 1675 at the age of 80. His homestead was burned down during King Philip's War and was never rebuilt.

---

test laws that persecuted Quakers. At one point, William Robinson and Marmaduke Stephenson were arrested in Boston for heresy after having been previously banished from the colony. Dyer went to visit her friends and was also arrested (she, too, had been previously told not to return to the colony). The three were sentenced to death. This time, Robinson and Stephenson were hanged, but Dyer received a last-minute reprieve and was set free with the condition that she leave Boston for good.

In 1660, Dyer so believed in the right of freedom of religion that she returned to Massachusetts even though her family begged her not to. Arrested and convicted once again, Mary Dyer was given one last chance at the gallows to repent and be again banished. She refused and was hanged. Her last words were, "Nay, I came to keep bloodguiltiness from you, desireing you to repeal the unrighteous and unjust law made against the innocent servants of the Lord. Nay, man, I am not now to repent." She is buried in Newport, Rhode Island. Be sure to check out the statue erected in her honor outside the Massachusetts State House.

Also executed on the Common were **Margaret Jones** and **Mistress Anne Hibbins,** who were expunged from the Divine State for being proven consorts of His Satanic Majesty. For unspecified crimes against the settlers, **Matoonas,** an Algonquian Indian sagamore, or subordinate chief, was tied to a tree and shot in 1656. These gruesome occasions were declared general holidays and attracted great crowds on the Common.

The land was also used as a military parade ground for the local "trayn-band," or militia. Before and during the early years of the Revolution, British regiments encamped on Boston Common.

It wasn't always violent on the Common, however. In 1824, when **General Lafayette** made his goodwill trip to the young democracy, Boston's schoolchildren turned out on the Common to sing "La Marseillaise." The general was also honored by 1,200 people at a public banquet under a canopy on the Common.

The Common continued to evolve and was used as pastureland until 1830, when the animals were banished. The gallows were taken down in 1817. In the late 1820s, the Society for the Suppression of Intemperance convinced Mayor Harrison Gray Otis that he could

Located near the visitor's kiosk, Brewer Fountain received its name from Gardener Brewer, who donated the sculpture in 1868. PHOTO BY STEPHEN W. PIETRZYK

"promote order and suppress an inclination to riot and intemperance" by holding municipal concerts on the Common. Ever since, music lovers have gathered in the shade of towering oaks for band concerts and crowded under moonlit skies for performances by popular entertainers.

The 20th century brought its own movers and shakers. The **Reverend Martin Luther King Jr.** addressed thousands on the Common in 1965 and **Pope John Paul II** celebrated a public Mass here in 1979. **Gloria Steinem** advanced the feminist revolution on these grounds at the turn of the 21st century, The **Massachusetts Cannabis Reform Coalition** presented their Annual Boston Freedom Rally in 1992 (although they have had to fight for the right), **Cindy Sheehan** addressed antiwar protesters in 2005, in 2008 Bostonians gathered on the Common to make a stand against the War in Iraq, former Republican vice presidential candidate **Sarah Palin** called for lower taxes and less government at a Tea Party Rally on the Common in Spring 2010, and in October of 2010, more than a hundred people converged on the Common to attend a satellite rally by Comedy Central comedians **Jon Stewart** and **Stephen Colbert** who hosted the "Rally to Restore Sanity And/Or Fear" in Washington, D.C. Those are just a few of the countless groups and individuals who have used this wonderful piece of America's history as the backdrop for their platform.

With all its contemporary appeal, the Common continues to pay tribute to the past by providing a setting for many notable sculptures. The **Soldiers and Sailors Monument,** whose figures personify history and peace, rises like a vision from a hilltop. **Brewer Fountain** stands tall just steps from the visitor's kiosk. Donated by Gardner Brewer in 1868, it depicts the mythical figures of Neptune, Galatea, Amphitrite, and Acis. The palette-shaped monument just within the fence of the Central Burying Ground at the corner of Tremont and Boylston Streets honors painter Gilbert Stuart, who is buried in one of the unmarked graves.

The most famous sculpture is undoubtedly the **Robert Gould Shaw and Fifty-fourth Regiment Memorial** by Augustus Saint-Gaudens at the corner of Park and Beacon Streets, facing the State House. This bronze memorial commemorates the bravery of the first black regiment to be recruited in the North. Their colonel, the 26-year-old Robert Gould Shaw, son of a prominent Boston family who had volunteered for the assignment, and half of his regiment perished in the attack on Fort Wagner, South Carolina, in July 1863. The 1989 film *Glory* tells the story of the regiment's heroism. For more information on this memorial, visit www.afroammuseum.org/site1.htm.

The long mall running from Beacon Street at the Joy Street entrance across the whole length of the Common to the corner of Boylston and Tremont Streets is called the **Oliver Wendell Holmes**

The Soldiers and Sailors Monument on Boston Common memorializes all those who stood up for what they believed in. PHOTO BY STEPHEN W. PIETRZYK

Walk. The eminent physician and writer recalled walking here with Amelia Lee Jackson: "I think I tried to speak twice without making myself distinctly audible. At last I got out the question—Will you take the long path with me?—Certainly,—said the schoolmistress,—with much pleasure—Think,—I said,—before you answer; if you take the long path with me now, I shall interpret it that we are to part no more. She answered softly, I will walk the long path with you!"

Many prominent and notable characters have walked the paths since. **Walt Whitman** and **Ralph Waldo Emerson** walked together for two hours on May 12, 1863, perhaps it was here that the Sage of Concord used all of his powers of persuasion, without success, to convince Whitman to delete "The Children of Adam" portion of *Leaves of Grass.*

In the 1600s no one strolled the Common on Sunday; it was a day reserved for serious churchgoing. Today, Sunday is the Common's day to shine. Easter Sunday especially finds Boston families strutting their finery on the Common. And on warm summer days, strolling the Common offers relief from the city's parched pavement. Office workers enjoy picnic lunches here. Retirees relax on benches. Children splash in **Frog Pond** in summer and ice-skate in winter. Year-round, people hand-feed friendly pigeons and squirrels.

History meets modern convenience beneath the park's pastoral setting, where there's a 1,300-car parking garage, and at the **corner of Park and Tremont Streets** is the entrance to the oldest subway in America. This corner has also been the site of memorable events, including the world's largest craps game, during the Boston police strike of 1919, and Vietnam War protests. The tradition continues, and the Common remains a popular spot for soapbox orators, who provide entertaining street theater with their passionate commentary.

Side Trip: Site of the Liberty Tree

A few blocks off the Freedom Trail, at the corner of Washington and Essex Streets sits a plaque that marks the place where the Patriots' famed **Liberty Tree** once stood. The plaque is about a block east of Boylston T Station on the third story of the Registry of Motor Vehicles building, above the Chinatown T stop. The official address is 630 Washington St. If you are starting your walk at Boston Common, you're going to have to go south along Tremont Street to Boylston Station, then turn left onto Essex Street and walk east about 1 block to the intersection of Washington Street. Note that when you're at the corner of Tremont and Essex Street, it's Essex Street to your left, but it's Boylston to your right, the street changes its name as it crosses Tremont. Phew! Good luck!

Once you find the plaque, or even if you don't, consider this: The Liberty Tree played a pivotal role in the colonists' fight for independence when it was chosen by the Sons of Liberty as the tree from which to hang an **effigy of Andrew Oliver,** the Royal stamp collector. The **Stamp Act** was levied by the British Parliament in 1765 to help defray the cost of defending the American frontier. It taxed newspapers and various official and legal documents.

The colonists interpreted this tax as a flagrant example of taxation without representation, and Boston was in an uproar. One response was the formation of the group who called themselves the **Sons of Liberty.** Groups formed throughout the colonies with one of their common objectives being to convince stamp collectors to resign from their posts. Any merchant who was found in compliance with the Stamp Act might find himself visited by the group as well. True to their cause, members of the Boston Sons of Liberty hanged Oliver in effigy at daybreak on August 14.

Word of the "hanging" spread, and soon thousands of people gathered at the spot to express their admiration and approval. At dusk the crowd took down the effigy, placed it on a funeral bier, and formed a vast torchlight procession to the stamp office, which they promptly tore apart. The mob then built a bonfire and cremated the effigy. The next day the real Mr. Oliver, who was also the brother-in-law of the colony's lieutenant governor, Thomas Hutchinson, was compelled to appear under the gallows of the Liberty Tree and to renounce his duties as stamp officer.

On September 11, a plate with the inscription THE TREE OF LIBERTY was placed on the trunk, and the Sons of Liberty continued to meet here. The British soldiers, knowing what the elm tree meant to the colonists,

Mob Mentality

While **Samuel Adams** was an expert at inciting crowds, he and the others soon came to realize that large, unruly crowds could pose problems. Now that the Liberty Tree was becoming known as *the* place to meet, and other colonies were selecting their own Liberty Trees, those in the forefront of the fight for freedom found themselves with little or no control of who or how many came to these meetings. Often, the topics of these meetings (and most likely a plethora of spirits) would incite the crowds into forming unruly mobs with justice on their minds. Such was the case one evening in late August 1765 when the story goes that one such mob built a bonfire on King's Street (today's State Street) and proceeded to attack and ransack the homes of various royal officials, including the governor's residence, which was reduced to a mere shell while several hundred people watched, doing nothing. The next morning Samuel Adams was quick to distance himself from the events, saying the work was that of "a lawless unknown rabble."

continually ridiculed it. A year later, during the siege of Boston, they defiantly cut it down. A contemporary journalist reported, "After a long spell of laughing and grinning, sweating and swearing, and foaming with malice diabolical [British soldiers] cut down a tree because it bore the name of liberty."

After having stood for more than one hundred years, witness to the birth of freedom, the tree was reduced to a stump. The patriots of Boston, however, renamed it the **Liberty Stump** and continued to use it as a place of assembly.

For years the site of the Liberty Tree went unnoticed. An old plaque that had been hung to mark the spot sat grimy and forgotten. Then, in 1966, a newspaper reporter went on a quest to find the old plaque and was disturbed to find it in such a condition. He contacted then governor John A. Volpe to visit the site in hopes that something could be done. Volpe visited the site and pledged his assistance. Eventually, a bronze replica of the plaque was created by the Boston Redevelopment Authority and installed in the plaza at the intersection of Boylston and Washington Streets where it remains today.

MASSACHUSETTS STATE HOUSE

Beacon and Park Streets

The **Massachusetts State House,** begun in 1795 and completed in 1798, is the crowning achievement of **Charles Bulfinch,** who also designed Connecticut's State House and was the architect for the Capitol in Washington, D.C.

After returning from an architectural tour abroad, Bulfinch submitted his design for the Massachusetts capitol in November 1787. He explained that it was "in the style of a building celebrated all over Europe," London's Somerset House on the banks of the Thames, a monumental neo-Palladian government building by Sir William Chambers. More than seven years elapsed before the design was implemented, however, and **Samuel Adams** and **Paul Revere** laid the cornerstone on July 4, 1795.

The State House originally was intended for a site on the lower part of the Common, but Bulfinch had begun to design and build handsome residences near **John Hancock'**s mansion atop Beacon Hill, so the location was changed to this more fashionable part of town. For two and a half years, the architect supervised masons, carpenters, plasterers, carvers, painters, glaziers, and roofers. Progress was slow, expenses high; but when the State House was completed, it was praised as "the most magnificent building in the Union," a marvel of "perfect taste and proportion."

The original redbrick facade, now enlarged by two wings, generally resembles the pavilion of Lord Somerset's house; in detail, however, it is an original neoclassical Bulfinch composition. The famous **golden dome,** 50 feet in diameter and 30 feet high, is a grand, dominating hemisphere. It is topped by a cupola and a pinecone, a symbol of the lumber

> ### The Beacon Hill Monument
> **Beacon Hill Monument,** facing Ashburton Place behind the State House, pays tribute to the original monument that used to stand on **Sentry Hill.**
>
> When the first settlers arrived, Boston had three hills— Sentry Hill, Mount Vernon, and Cotton Hill. On Sentry Hill, the highest, settlers erected a tall pole with rungs all the way up. On top of this lookout, they filled a pot with pitch and pinewood. In times of danger—fire or attack by Indians or British troops—they could set a fire to warn the inhabitants of the town.
>
> When the old structure blew down in 1789, Charles Bulfinch proposed a monument "to commemorate the train of events which led to the American Revolution."
>
> He was then was commissioned to design it, and it became Boston's first Revolutionary War monument. Erected in 1791, the stuccoed brick and stone monument was 60 feet tall and topped with an eagle. In 1811, however, Beacon Hill's crest was removed for landfill and the column came down.
>
> A copy of the monument, incorporating its original tablets, was built in 1865 and stands today on the present site.

industry and Maine, which at the time was part of Massachusetts. First built of wood, the grand dome didn't exactly stand up to New England weather; it started to leak rather quickly. Something had to be done and done quickly, so in 1802 Paul Revere and Sons sheathed the dome in copper and it was painted a lead gray. It was later painted yellow for about 20 years before being returned to its gray color and then finally gilded with 14-karat gold leaf in 1874, and more recently in 1997.

Enoch Cobb Wines, a 19th-century travel writer, reported on the view from the dome in his letters to the *United States Gazette*. "I speak soberly and without exaggeration," he wrote. "There are few prospects either in the new world or the old that can be compared to this."

The interior was just as handsome. Lofty ceilings, ornamental plasterwork by **Daniel Raynard,** and the richly carved columns and

Except for a period during World War II when it was blacked out, the gold dome of the State House has gleamed for more than a century. PHOTO BY STEPHEN W. PIETRZYK

Old vs. New

Even though this State House is more than 200 years old, it is referred to as the "new" State House in order to differentiate from the "Old" State House located on the corner of Congress and State Streets, which is almost a hundred years older.

---

pilasters of the principal rooms were universally admired. Portraits of Massachusetts governors now hang in the entrance hall. Above the entrance hall to the visitors' gallery hangs the 200-year-old, 5-foot-long **Sacred Cod.** This pinewood fish symbolizes the importance of the fishing industry to Massachusetts. During meetings, the Speaker of the House faces this historic symbol. No one was looking, however, in 1933 when the wooden cod was "cod-napped" as a prank by some college students. It remained missing for a couple of days until it was returned to its rightful place after an anonymous tip alerted police to its whereabouts.

Although the State House has been enlarged greatly and the interior extensively remodeled, the Bulfinch front remains intact, an authentic American temple to democracy.

Step to the Side, Please
The center doors of the State House are opened only for governors when they depart at the end of their terms, for the president of the United States or foreign heads of state, or when Massachusetts Regimental Flags are received. The public should enter and leave through the side doors.

After the State House was built, town fathers decided it would look more impressive without Boston's hills around it. **Mount Vernon,** to the west, was used to fill the river and raise Charles Street. In 1845 **Cotton Hill,** on the east, was leveled and used to fill a millpond at its foot. This endeavor created 8 acres of downtown land, including the site of the **Court House.**

By a twist of fate, the private fortune of Charles Bulfinch was sinking just as his public reputation reached its height. Committing nearly all of his wealth to an ambitious residential development known as the Tontine Crescent on Franklin Street, Bulfinch was unable to weather one of the many financial panics of the early Republic. In 1799, unwilling to see its great citizen reduced to poverty, Boston elected him chief selectman and superintendent of police. As the town's leading administrator/architect, he improved nearly every aspect of his native place, from the execution of laws and the conduct of government to the planning and laying out of new streets and the design of dozens of residential, commercial, ecclesiastical, and institutional buildings.

Site of John Hancock's House

John Hancock's house, which stood on what is now the west lawn of the State House, was torn down in 1863. One of the last of the great Georgian mansions in Boston, as notable architecturally as it was historically, it was built in 1737 for John's uncle Thomas Hancock, a wealthy merchant who had started out as a bookbinder and stationer.

Two stories high and constructed of Connecticut stone brought to Boston by boat, the mansion boasted a gambrel roof, corner quoins, four large chimneys, an elegant rooftop captain's walk, and a richly paneled interior—all in all, the house of an English squire. For 30 years, until painter John Singleton Copley built his mansion, the Hancock house stood in solitary splendor among formal gardens and fruit trees on the side of old Beacon Hill, overlooking the green expanse of the Common.

On Thomas's death in 1764, nephew John, then a high-living young dandy who was just beginning to espouse the cause of liberty, inherited.

Now having a fortune—particularly helpful to someone who was not adept at commerce—John Hancock plunged into the revolutionary politics of the day. He served as moderator of the Boston town meeting, sat as a member of the town's various rebel committees, and later became president of both the Massachusetts Revolutionary Congress and the Continental Congress in Philadelphia.

British soldiers occupied the house at the time of the signing of the Declaration of Independence, a fact that some suggest accounts for the boldness of Hancock's signature. George III had put a price on Hancock's head. When Hancock became the first signer of the Declaration of Independence, he rendered his autograph with a conspicuous flourish and declared, "John Bull can read that without spectacles! Now let him double his reward!"

Hancock served as first governor of Massachusetts, and at the end of his life he attempted to donate his house to the Commonwealth for a museum of the Revolution or a governor's mansion. The Commonwealth declined. Even after his heirs persisted, the gift was refused, and so the house was torn down. Today a plaque stands to commemorate the spot where the house once stood.

A replica of the Hancock mansion has been created in New York. For more information, visit www.thehancockhouse.org.

Given Bulfinch's lifetime of extraordinary accomplishment, it is difficult to assign preeminence to any one of his projects; and yet the State House is regarded as Bulfinch's masterpiece. In one magnificent stroke he introduced a new architecture for the new nation, powerful and majestic, expressive of the ideals embodied in the Constitution of a self-governing people. America's first professional architect set a new standard and applied it to every aspect of Boston—a legacy of excellence that endures to this day.

State House Information

Hours: 10 a.m. to 4 p.m. Mon through Fri; closed weekends and holidays

Admission: Free; 35- to 40-minute tours are given year-round and are also free, but reservations are required

Phone: (617) 727-3676

Wheelchair accessibility: Bowdoin Street, front right corner of building, and the Ashburton Park entrance off Bowdoin Street near rear of building

Be aware when you visit the State House that all regulations and restrictions that pertain to federal buildings apply here as well.

PARK STREET CHURCH

Corner of Tremont and Park Streets

Still operating today with a strong Evangelical congregation, the elegant **Park Street Church,** erected in 1809 on the site of Boston's Old Granary, dominates its streetscape. It is a masterpiece of ecclesiastical architecture and, according to American novelist Henry James, "the most interesting mass of brick and mortar in America."

Peter Banner, the church's English architect, had recently arrived in Boston from Connecticut, where he had designed buildings for Yale University. Banner drew on nearly every element of **Charles Bulfinch**'s residential design vocabulary, infused it with the grace of **Sir Christopher Wren**'s London spires, and produced an edifice so striking and so enduring that the Trinitarian Evangelical congregation has never left.

Although the lofty steeple was shortened after a bad spell of swaying in the 19th century, Park Street Church has been carefully preserved and still presents an extremely graceful facade, with bowfront

---

The Place of Firsts

The first Sunday school was organized at Park Street Church in 1816.

The first Protestant missionaries to Hawaii were dispatched from this church in 1819.

On Independence Day 1831 Samuel Francis Smith's song "America," also known as "My Country 'Tis of Thee," was first sung here

Lowell Mason, leading figure in American church music and composer of many well-known and still-used-today hymns was Park Street Church's first organist.

Now standing tall over Boston, Park Street Church's steeple once had to be shortened to avoid swaying. PHOTO BY STEPHEN W. PIETRZYK

colonnades, a Palladian tower window, recessed arches, a pedimented belfry, a towering steeple, and carved wood detail by Boston's **Solomon Willard,** architect of the **Bunker Hill Monument.**

Despite its superior commercial site in the heart of downtown Boston, the church has never been endangered by possible sale or demolition. During a period of financial difficulty, however, part of the building was rented out as a tearoom, until it was discovered that women were displeasing the Lord by smoking cigarettes!

Park Street Church is no stranger to controversy. On the Fourth of July, 1829, **William Lloyd Garrison,** the great abolitionist and publisher of the *Liberator,* gave his first public antislavery address— an oration not well received by his audience, who at one point tried to lynch him. And in 1849 **Charles Sumner** delivered his powerful oration, "The War System of Nations," to the American Peace Society.

In part as recognition of the many hellfire-and-brimstone sermons thundered from its pulpit, and in part because brimstone was stored in the church's cellar during the War of 1812, the corner of Park and Tremont Streets is known as **Brimstone Corner.**

Park Street Church Information

Hours: 9 a.m. to 4 p.m. Tues through Fri, and Sat 9 a.m. to 3 p.m., late June through Aug. Winter hours by appointment only. Sunday services are held year-round at 8:30 a.m., 11 a.m., 4 p.m., and 6:30 p.m.

Admission: Free. Visitors can view a video on the history of the Park Street Church and guided and self-guided tours are available.

Phone: (617) 523-3383

Website: www.parkstreet.org

Wheelchair accessibility: Yes, ramp on the Park Street side of building. Visit the website above and click on "directions and parking" to be linked to a detailed information sheet on accessibility to the church and some on Boston in general.

GRANARY BURYING GROUND

Tremont Street, Near Park Street Church

> For nearly three hundred years it has kept its hallowed
> peace. Its headstones are little and dull, and covered
> with moss. And the trees that shelter them are grim
> and old. And, after dark, the little night winds sob as
> they tiptoe through the gloom.
>
> —*Eleanor Early,* This Is Boston, *1930*

The **Granary Burying Ground** was established in 1660 on land that
was part of Boston Common. "There is a lovely solemnity about this
little cemetery," noted **Eleanor Early** in her 1930 book, *This Is Bos-*
ton. The cemetery was meant to ease crowding at the **King's Chapel**
Burying Ground and takes its name from the wooden building used
to store wheat and other grains, which used to stand on the spot now
occupied by the **Park Street Church.** Since the granary was torn
down and the beautiful Park Street Church erected, the church's lithe
lines provide contrast to the Burying Ground's heavily symbolic granite
gate with its winged globe and downturned torches.

More than 2,000 graves are located here. In addition to ordinary
men, women, and children who pioneered the little world of Boston,
scores of **Revolutionary War soldiers;** the city's first mayor, **John**
Phillips; and the **five Boston Massacre victims** are buried here.
In fact, **Samuel Adams** requested that they be buried in his family's
tomb; you'll see the marker next to his tomb. This is also the final resting place of three signers of the Declaration of Independence—**John**
Hancock, Samuel Adams, and **Robert Treat Paine**—along with

eight governors; philanthropist **Peter Faneuil,** ("Funel" on his flat stone); diarist **Judge Samuel Sewall,** who lived to repent his part in the witchcraft trials; **Paul Revere;** and **Benjamin Franklin's parents,** whose graves are marked with the original stone and an obelisk erected by the citizens of Boston.

Still Together

Funerals were (and are) expensive. Many families could not afford a headstone for each member who died. According to the CityofBoston.gov website, approximately 5,000 people (some sources say more) are buried at the Granary Burying Ground; there are only 2,300 headstones. Each grave can contain as many as 20 bodies.

Among old graveyards with their illustrious dead, their quaint inscriptions, and above all their sense of repose, Granary Burying Ground is unsurpassed. Many 17th-century stones still stand, richly lettered and carved with ghastly death's heads and emblems of the fruits of paradise, Puritan symbols of the departing soul and the blissful eternity that is its destination. Since the Puritan church did not believe in or approve of religious imagery, these headstones were often the outlet for artistic expression. The oldest marker in the cemetery belongs to **Hannah Allen;** the oldest upright stone, to **John Wakefield.**

The burying ground harbors some lesser-known but interesting characters, too. **Ann Pollard,** a child when she arrived with the first settlers, was the first to hop ashore at Shawmutt, later known as Boston. She grew up, married, and gave birth to numerous children. Surviving her husband by decades, she followed an independent, pipe-smoking course and operated the wild-and-woolly Horse Shoe Tavern. At the age of 103, she had her portrait painted. When she died two years later, the whole town joined her hundred-plus descendants in mourning her.

This obelisk guards the graves of Benjamin Franklin's parents. Franklin himself is buried in Philadelphia, Pennsylvania. PHOTO BY STEPHEN W. PIETRZYK

Benjamin Woodbridge found his way into this resting place in 1728. He made an injudicious remark at the Royal Exchange, the merchants' gathering place, and was challenged to a duel with swords. He accepted. The affair of honor, held on Boston Common, ended with a rapier running through the young man.

The story of **Elisha Brown** is etched on his stone. He prevented an entire regiment of His Majesty's troops from dispossessing him of his spacious home, which they coveted as a barracks. He held the regiment off for 17 days before they decided to leave him alone.

The Granary Burying Ground was the recipient of a $300,000 restoration project in the spring of 2011. After more than 350 years, the grounds were showing a little wear. The upgrades were intended to protect this hallowed ground of history for many generations to come.

Granary Burying Ground Information

Hours: 9:30 a.m. to 3:30 p.m. Tues through Sat, mid-June through Aug.

Admission: Free

Phone: Boston Parks Department, (617) 635-4504

Wheelchair accessibility: Limited; 4 steps to enter in front, but northeast side gate (down an alley off Beacon Street) has ramp

Please, no grave rubbings.

KING'S CHAPEL AND BURYING GROUND

58 Tremont Street

King's Chapel sits majestically at the corner of School and Tremont Streets. The large columned front is sure to catch your attention as you wander the Trail. However, as sometimes happens, this chapel ended up as something quite different from what its controversial beginnings would have indicated. It began in 1686, when **King James II** charged the despotic **Royal Governor Sir Edmund Andros** with building an Anglican church in New England. However, townsfolk had no use for such a church and refused to sell him land. Not to be deterred, the governor appropriated a corner of the Puritan town's first graveyard for a small wood chapel, complete with spire, to house the first Anglican congregation in New England.

Sentiment against Andros had been building, and this affront provoked such strong hostility from the colonists that he was forced to flee. But King's Chapel remained in all its splendor. Royal officials continued to worship in handsome style, surrounded by opulent decoration. In 1696, King William gifted the communion table in memory of Queen Mary, and another patron sent the Chancel tablets, all of which are still in use today. Dukes and earls donated silver service. Queen Anne and King George III also favored the church with gifts of silver and vestments.

The congregation grew, and in 1710 the building was enlarged. By 1741 Boston's Anglicans had decided to replace the old wood chapel with a London-style stone edifice, but the project was deferred until 1748, when funds were raised. The congregation retained the talents of **Peter Harrison,** a gentleman designer from Newport, Rhode Island.

The colonnaded portico was added to King's Chapel in 1790. While these columns appear to be made of granite, they are actually wood. PHOTO BY STEPHEN W. PIETRZYK

Harrison's final design called for a substantial stone building and tower, to be lightened by the "beautiful effect" of a lofty wood steeple. He also proposed a double row of windows, the lower smaller than the upper, causing one wit to comment that he "had heard of the Cannons of the Church, but had never before seen the portholes."

When **Governor William Shirley** laid the cornerstone for the new edifice in August 1749, angry Puritans threw garbage. Nevertheless, great blocks of rough-hewn stonewalls soon rose around the existing wood chapel. Services continued to be held inside the wood chapel while construction was going on outside until 1753, at which time the walls of the smaller chapel were demolished and thrown, piece by piece, out the windows of its successor. The pulpit and under flooring of that original wooden church are still in use today.

Eventually, money ran out, and the "beautiful effect" of Peter Harrison's steeple was never realized. Yet the interior of the new church was a marvel of Georgian elegance, and when the building was completed in 1754, the Anglicans were pleased.

During the siege of Boston, British military and naval officers worshiped here. With the hasty departure of the Tories, Boston removed the King from the chapel and rechristened it **Stone Chapel.** The name didn't last.

In 1790, shortly after **George Washington** attended an oration, the colonnaded portico was added. The final change took place in 1785, when the first Anglican church in New England became the first Unitarian church in America.

Remember Pierre

When you enter Kings Chapel, you may notice a basket of buttons on a table near the door. The buttons read: REMEMBER PIERRE, KING'S CHAPEL, BOSTON 1686. Why do you need to remember Pierre? Because, quite frankly, he was forgotten for long enough. You see, Pierre was a cousin of the King of France who felt sympathetic toward the colonists. As French lieutenant, he decided he would come to America and help fight the revolution. Alas, however, things didn't quite go his way. He was killed, not in battle, but in a bar brawl before he could do much to help the cause. Pierre was then buried in King Chapel's Strangers' Tomb in a secret Catholic ceremony. A monument and a grand funeral were promised, but with everything going on, poor Pierre was ultimately forgotten by the US government. The French, however, did not forget forever. About a hundred years ago, the French government reminded the powers that be in the United States of their promise. We made good on our word and a monument was erected in Pierre's honor and now stands in the Chapel's courtyard. So, when in Boston, please stop and pay your respects to dear Pierre, the Frenchman who wanted to be a Revolutionary.

Today, King's Chapel is an independent Christian Church whose congregation follows a Unitarian Christian Theology. Regular services are still held throughout the year on Sunday and Wednesday.

When a service is not in session, the church is open to visitors. Upon entering the double doors of the church, you'll be greeted by guides who are there to answer any of your questions. There's an informative pamphlet that you can use as you explore the church. Don't be afraid to engage the guides, they are a wealth of information and are eager to share.

Inside the church you'll find the large pew boxes, which colonial families would own and decorate at their whimsy. Today, most of them have been redecorated uniformly and are no longer individually owned. They are, however, quite comfortable, which was important, as one guide pointed out, because the services were likely to last for up to four hours and parents could be fined if their children fidgeted too much! As you look around, take note of the organ up in the gallery. It is quite impressive. It is the church's sixth organ and was made by **C.B. Fisk.**

Don't be fooled by the Church's size, take your time to enjoy the tour and spend some time with the guides. You'll be glad you did. And don't forget to ask about Pierre.

King's Chapel Burying Ground

For thirty years this was Boston's only burying ground. In September 1630 **Sir Isaac Johnson,** a leader of the **Massachusetts Bay Company,** succumbed to the rigors of the New World and was buried in the southwest corner of his garden lot. As other Puritans planned for their demises, they asked to be buried alongside Brother Johnson.

King's Chapel Burying Ground is the final resting place of nearly the entire first generation of Boston's English settlers. The oldest gravestone remaining here belongs to **Deacon William Paddy,** who died in 1658. The Massachusetts Bay Colony's first governor,

King's Chapel Burying Ground is the final resting place of nearly the entire first generation of Boston's English settlers. PHOTO BY STEPHEN W. PIETRZYK

John Winthrop, and **Elizabeth Pain,** whose headstone is said to have inspired **Nathaniel Hawthorne** as he wrote *The Scarlet Letter,* are interred here, too. **Mary Chilton,** who arrived with the Pilgrims on the Mayflower and is credited as being the first Englishwoman to set foot in New England, is here, too, as are the pastors of the First Church and other early notables.

The present arrangement of the headstones is the work of an old-time superintendent of burials. He apparently considered the beautifully carved old slates to be elements of a composition (his), rather than accurate grave markers.

King's Chapel Information

Hours: 10 a.m. to 4 p.m. most days, except Sun, when the hours are 1 to 4 p.m. The Chapel is also closed from 11:30 a.m. to 1 p.m. on Tues and Wed. The burying ground is open 9 a.m. to 5 p.m. daily, except it closes at 3 p.m. during winter

Admission: $1 donation is suggested for the church; the Burying Ground is free

Phone: Church, (617) 523-1749; Burying Ground, (617) 635-4505

Website: www.kings-chapel.org

Wheelchair accessibility: Main floor of church partially accessible. One pew box is also handicapped accessible.

SITE OF THE FIRST PUBLIC SCHOOL

School Street

The **Boston Latin School,** established by Puritans on April 13, 1635, and still operating today, is the country's oldest public school. Originally having no formal building, classes were held at the home of headmaster **Philemon Pormont.** Later, a wooden structure was built on School Street, just to the right of Lilli Ann Killen Rosenberg's *City Center,* a colorful mosaic set into the sidewalk to mark the location. Brass letters, Venetian glass, and ceramic pieces spell out the names of the school's famous alumni, including **Samuel Adams, Cotton Mather,** and **John Hancock.** The school building was completed in 1645 on Tremont Street and existed peacefully for a hundred years. In 1745 the school moved to this location on School Street and the enlarged **King's Chapel** took over the land it once occupied. The school existed in that location until 1812, when it was moved to another location on School Street. The school went through a few more moves before settling in its current location in the Fenway neighborhood of Boston, where it continues to thrive. Other notable graduates of BLS have included **Henry Ward Beecher, Leonard Bernstein, Charles Bulfinch, Ralph Waldo Emerson, Edward Everett, Joseph Kennedy, Henry Knox, Wendell Phillips, Josiah Quincy,** and **Charles Sumner. Benjamin Franklin** and **Louis Farrakhan** also attended, but didn't graduate. Girls were not allowed to attend until 1972.

Also near the former site of the Boston Latin School on the grounds of the old City Hall are two statues. If you stand on the mosaic and look toward the old City Hall, you'll find **Benjamin Franklin** on your left and **Josiah Quincy** on your right. They are both Boston Latin School alums and were instrumental in Boston at the time of the Revolution.

He Said, He Said

During the time leading up to the war and through the Revolution, many family members found themselves on different sides of the war. This was true in the Lovell family. John Lovell Sr. was a former assistant teacher at the Boston Latin School who eventually succeeded Dr. Nathaniel Williams as headmaster. Years later, Lovell's son James was appointed assistant teacher. Things then got a little tense, albeit educational for sure. You see, Lovell Jr. was an ardent patriot, whereas Lovell Sr. was a strong loyalist. They taught from desks at opposite ends of the schoolroom often voicing opposite political convictions.

The men, however, stayed true to their beliefs through the tumultuous times in the city. When the British troops left Boston in March of 1776, both Lovells sailed with Lord Howe to Halifax, Nova Scotia. Lovell Sr. as Howe's guest, Lovell Jr. as his prisoner, having been imprisoned after the Battle of Bunker Hill. Younger Lovell was later exchanged for a British solder and eventually became a delegate to the Continental Congress. The Elder Lovell died at Halifax in 1778.

Erected in 1856, the **8-foot-tall bronze statue of Benjamin Franklin** was fashioned by **Richard Saltonstall Greenough** and is Boston's first public portrait statue. In executing the commission, the sculptor observed that he "found the left of the great man's face philosophical and reflective, and the right side funny and smiling." Tablets on the base recall scenes from Franklin's life.

Franklin, while receiving his few years of formal schooling and a taste for books at Boston Latin School, was largely self-taught. He excelled as a printer, writer, editor, inventor, scientist, military officer, politician, and statesman. He is the only American who signed all four of the critical documents in Revolutionary-era history: the Declaration of Independence, the Treaty of Alliance with France, the treaty of peace with Great Britain, and the Constitution of the United States.

Erected in 1856, this statue of Benjamin Franklin stands outside the Old City Hall on the site of his former school, and is Boston's first public portrait statue. PHOTO BY STEPHEN W. PIETRZYK

The **statue of Josiah Quincy** was designed by **Thomas Ball** and erected in 1879. Josiah Quincy served as Boston's mayor from 1823 to 1829. He was also an author and educator who went on to become a member of the Massachusetts Senate and the US Congress, and president of Harvard University.

While mayor of Boston, Quincy was ahead of his time with respect to his vision for the city. What we might call urban renewal today, Quincy was implementing in the nineteenth century. He is largely responsible for revitalizing the tidal land that now holds **Faneuil Hall Marketplace.** (See **Faneuil Hall** chapter on p. 65 for more information.)

BLS Information

Phone: (617) 635-4505

Website: www.cityofboston.gov

Side Trip: Old City Hall

The construction of Boston's **Old City Hall** began in 1862 and continued for three years. Designed by **Gridley J.F. Bryan** and **Arthur Gilman,** this majestic building served as Boston's official city hall from 1865 through 1969. In 1969, the current city hall was built at **Government Center** and Old City Hall's future was changed. Even though it was not yet in practice to convert old buildings for other uses, that's exactly what happened. Old City Hall (45 School St.) was successfully converted into an office building, complete with a restaurant. It was one of the first examples of this sort of reuse of such a building. In 1970, the building was designated a National Historic Landmark and has since received numerous awards for the brilliant architecture and the strides taken to preserve it. For more information, visit www.oldcityhall.com or call (617) 523-8678.

OLD CORNER BOOKSTORE

3 School Street, Corner of Washington Street

In 1712, a year after fire had destroyed the neighborhood, **Thomas Crease** built this solid brick house as his residence and Boston's first apothecary shop. With its steep gambrel roof, brick belt courses, and corner quoins, the English-style town house was one of the handsomest in the community of about 10,000 people.

The Crease house became a bookstore when **Timothy Carder** opened shop in 1829. In the early to mid 1800s, **William D. Ticknor** and **James T. Fields** were entering the world of publishing. Ticknor, a resourceful young man, obtained the rights to publish works of British authors by adopting the then novel practice of paying royalties. Fields was a book clerk who astonished his colleagues by correctly predicting, as soon as they entered the shop, what books customers would buy.

A Glass of Red?
In the mid-1800s, which could be considered the Golden Age of American Literature, the former Crease house was the country's literary heart, an informal clubhouse where writers could always find good conversation and a glass of claret.

The two joined forces and from 1833 to 1864 **Ticknor and Fields, Inc.,** was the country's leading publisher. Its authors included **Henry Wadsworth Longfellow, Charles Dickens, Harriet Beecher Stowe, Nathaniel Hawthorne, Ralph Waldo Emerson, John Greenleaf Whittier, Oliver Wendell Holmes, Louisa May Alcott,** and **Henry David Thoreau.** *Walden,* "The Battle Hymn of the Republic," and the *Atlantic Monthly* were published here.

The building that became the Old Corner Bookstore stands at the corner of School and Washington Streets and has since 1712. PHOTO BY JONATHAN SEITZ

After Ticknor and Fields moved out, the building housed a number of different booksellers. By the mid-20th century, it had become a pizza parlor in a prime location for a new parking garage. With

---

Banished!

In the 1600s, the land on which Crease built his house almost a century later belonged to William Hutchinson. The Hutchinson's house was destroyed in a fire in 1711. Hutchinson's brilliant wife, Anne, ministered to the sick and held informal discussion groups for women in her home. Her controversial religious teachings challenged the male clergy and led to a dangerous Puritan schism, so the General Court (the Massachusetts legislature) banished her from the colony in the late 1630s. Anne Hutchinson took her husband and 14 children first to Rhode Island with Roger Williams, then to Pelham, New York, where, except for one daughter, all were killed by Indians.

encouragement from the city and financial assistance from the Boston Globe Newspaper Company, Historic Boston, Inc., purchased the run-down building in 1960 and restored it to its original appearance. A variety of tenants has called this historic building home ever since.

Side Trip: Ben Franklin's Birthplace & Print Shop

Although **Ben Franklin** is often associated with his adopted state of Pennsylvania, Massachusetts proudly claims him as a native son. One of our country's founding fathers, Franklin was born on January 17, 1706 at **17 Milk St.** A bust on the second story commemorates the site of the family home. To find the location, stand in front of the exit for the **Old South Meeting House Museum** and look directly across the street at the fancy white building, then look up. (At the time of our visit, a Sir Speedy shop was on the first floor.) Franklin's father, Josiah Franklin, married Ben's mother Abiah Foulger in 1689. She was his second wife and Ben was 15th of 17 children (he had 7 with first wife Anne Child).

When Ben was 8 years old, he attended the Boston Latin School. His father had hopes of him becoming a clergyman; however, the family's financial picture forced Ben to drop out after only a few months. He attended school elsewhere for a couple of years, but then dropped out completely at the age of 10. When he turned 12, he was apprenticed to his brother James at his **print shop.** A bronze tablet on the facade of the building that now houses the **New England Center for Homeless Veterans** at **17 Court St.** marks the place. James was the publisher of the *New England Courant,* and was a good newspaperman, seeming to know what his readers wanted to read. Young Ben's sprightly writing under the byline "Mrs. Silence Dogood" also contributed to the paper's success. Indeed, while at times unhappy with his brother's harsh treatment, Ben obtained a great deal of education during his apprenticeship. He set type by hand; absorbed the literary and political influences of the newspaper office and pressroom, and printed books, broadsides, and circulars, all of which he hawked on the street. "In a little time," he wrote, "I made great proficiency in the business, and became a useful hand to my brother."

James's outspoken style of writing, however, especially that of criticizing the church and the government, gave offense to the conservative legislature, and the Massachusetts General Court imprisoned him for a month. Ben ran the newspaper during his brother's absence and continued, as he put it, "to give our rulers some rubs in it." After James was released with the injunction he not print the *Courant,* the paper was published in Benjamin's name for several months.

Thank You, Ben!

In 1778 the Commonwealth of Massachusetts named a town in honor of the statesman, scholar, and humanist. To show his appreciation, Franklin considered giving his namesake either a church bell or a collection of books. Finally he decided on books. His reason, he said, was that "sense [is] more essential than sound." The books are still proudly showcased at the **Franklin Public Library** in an antique bookcase.

Eventually Ben, who had continually been looking for a way out of his apprenticeship, could take no more. James was an abusive brother and master. Ben resented him and later wrote, "His harsh and tyrannical treatment of me might be a means of impressing me with that aversion to arbitrary power that has stuck to me thro' my whole life."

Armed with a love of politics and writing, the self-reliant 17-year-old secured a release from his indenture, sold some of his books, and booked passage on a boat bound for New York, where he was unable to find employment as a printer and it was suggested he head to Philadelphia. In Philadelphia he became acquainted with the governor, who

This bust marks the place where Benjamin Franklin was born at 17 Milk St. The family home burned down in 1810. PHOTO BY STEPHEN W. PIETRZYK

offered to front him some money to start his own print shop. The governor suggested Franklin travel to London to purchase the equipment, but after spending weeks at sea, Franklin arrived in England to learn that the governor had failed to keep his promise; there was no money. The now 18-year-old spent two years in London before returning to Philadelphia in 1726. As a very skilled printer, Franklin was now able to start his own newspaper called *The Pennsylvania Gazette*. This paper made Franklin a rich man and brought him respect and influence; he was doing well. In 1730, Ben Franklin married Deborah Read and continued along quite well before retiring at the age of 42.

Once retired, Franklin was able to spend more time with his scientific experiments, eventually conducting his famous kite and key experiment in 1752 that proved that lightning and electricity were one and the same.

Dispensing with the Pleasantries

It is said that Franklin grew weary of people asking him about his travels. When he was younger and would arrive at a tavern, he would anticipate a query by saying, "My name is Benjamin Franklin. I was born in Boston. I am a printer by profession and am traveling to Philadelphia. I shall have to return at such and such a time, and I have no news. Now what can you give me for dinner?" He thought it would ensure his tranquility and gain immediate attention to his needs.

Franklin made so many important contributions to our country. When he died on April 17, 1790, at the age of 84, more than 20,000 people attended his funeral. He is buried in Christ Church Burial Ground in Philadelphia. His parents are buried in Boston.

OLD SOUTH MEETING HOUSE

310 Washington Street, Corner of Milk Street

Probably best known for the meeting place for the **Boston Tea Party** discussions, the **Old South Meeting House** has been witness to almost three centuries of history.

Built in 1729 as a Puritan meetinghouse, the structure was frequently used for mass gatherings and town meetings too large to fit into **Faneuil Hall**—some more controversial than others. And right up to the outbreak of the Revolution, Old South served as a rebel auditorium as well as a place of worship. In fact, Benjamin Franklin's family belonged to the congregation.

Because this building was so readily identified with the patriotic cause, the British troops took special revenge here. From June 1774 to June 1776, Old South was used as an officers' club and a riding academy, with a liquor dispensary in the gallery. Pieces of the interior were broken up for kindling. In the large open area thus created, several tons of dirt were dumped and raked smooth. It has been said that where the word of God and of man had rung out, the Queen's Light Dragoons spurred their mounts round and round, sometimes to drunken applause from the gallery above.

When the congregation regained control of their building in 1783, they restored the interior to its former state, including candlelight chandeliers and a white pulpit. The people of the town continued to hold overflow meetings here.

Twice Old South has nearly gone up in smoke. In December 1810 the roof caught fire, and the building seemed doomed. Fortunately the efforts of a courageous mastmaker, **Isaac Harris,** proved equal to the task. In gratitude for his extraordinary rooftop exertions, the **Third**

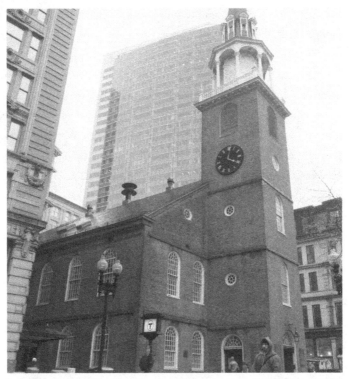
Built in 1729, the Old South Meeting House is best known as the meeting place for the Boston Tea Party discussions. PHOTO BY JONATHAN SEITZ

Religious Society presented him with an elegant silver water pitcher, which is now on display in the Boston Museum of Fine Arts.

Old South was threatened again when the **Great Boston Fire** in 1872 destroyed 65 acres of downtown Boston. The building was spared only to face demolition in the name of progress when the congregation sold the building and moved to its new location in Boston's Back Bay. The noble old building, located on a valuable commercial site, seemed destined for the wrecker's ball when Bostonians rallied once again. In a remarkable burst of civic pride, citizens, including Ralph Waldo Emerson, Mary Hemenway, Julia Ward Howe, Wendell

Phillips, and Louisa May Alcott successfully campaigned to stop the demolition. It is said to be the first example of urban historical preservation in New England. In 1877, Old South was incorporated as a history museum and historic site, and has continued as such ever since. Its venerable walls reverberate with the sounds of meetings, lectures, plays, concerts, memorial services, and church services. It is a living monument to the days and deeds of Adams, Quincy, Warren, and others who forged a revolution.

Old South Meeting House Information

Hours: 9:30 a.m. to 5 p.m. Apr 1 through Oct 31; 10 a.m. to 4 p.m. Nov 1 through Mar 31; closed Thanksgiving, Christmas Eve, Christmas Day, New Year's Day

Admission: Adults, $6; senior citizens and students with ID, $5; ages 6 to 18, $1. You may also purchase a discounted, multi-site ticket.

Phone: (617) 482-6439

Website: www.osmh.org

Wheelchair accessibility: Both Old South and the Museum Shop are wheelchair accessible

---

Side Trip: Boston Tea Party Ships & Museum

The largest and maybe the most famous assembly of the Revolutionary time occurred at the Old South Meeting House on the afternoon of December 16, 1773, when thousands of people crowded into the meetinghouse and thronged the streets outside to hear **Sam Adams** orate on the non-importation of certain British goods, particularly those to be found in the holds of three recently arrived merchant vessels.

Things had been heating up in the colonies. Britain kept pushing her rule and the colonists were pushing back harder and harder. Britain had levied taxes on items imported from England, forcing the colonists to pay taxes on staples such as sugar, tea, fabric, paper, coffee, and other items. There was the **Sugar Act of 1764,** the **Stamp Act of 1765,** and the dreaded **Townshend Acts of 1767.** Pushed too far, the colonists began to refuse to purchase these commodities, preferring to go without; which was not an easy task as we all know how much the English loved their tea. Even black mourning clothes ceased to be worn because black wool fabric came from England. This economic boycott so hurt the British that eventually the Townshend taxes were rescinded, save for the small tax on tea. The Crown was in the precarious position of not wanting to repeal all taxes lest they appear to accept the possibility that the colonists were right in their stand of "no taxation without representation." Then, as if to add insult to injury, Parliament passed the **Tea Act of 1773,** which allowed the **East India Tea Company** to avoid

---

Sam Adams . . .

. . . was born on September 27, 1722 in Boston

. . . had a father who was a brewer and merchant

. . . attended the Boston Latin School and Harvard Law School

. . . was second cousin to second US president John Adams

. . . was a Congregationalist

. . . was married twice and had six children, all with his first wife

. . . is considered to be the founder of the Sons of Liberty

. . . was a member of the Massachusetts Assembly and the Continental Congress, among others

. . . signed both the Declaration of Independence and the Articles of Confederation

. . . was governor of Massachusetts from 1794 to 1797

. . . died in 1803 at the age of 81

. . . is buried in Granary Burying Ground.

Sam Adams was an incredible force through the Revolutionary War. This statue outside Faneuil Hall memorializes the man. PHOTO BY STEPHEN W. PIETRZYK

paying the usual duties and tariffs as it left England. This allowed them to undersell other tea companies and further ignited the colonists.

When the **Eleanor, Dartmouth,** and **Beaver** entered Boston Harbor loaded with the East India Tea Company's cargo in early winter of that same year, the Royal Governor of Massachusetts Bay Colony, Thomas Hutchinson, insisted that they be unloaded and their cargoes sold according to the provisions of the Tea Act, including the payment of duties. The three ships sat anchored at Griffin's Wharf for more than a week while colonists tried to figure out what to do.

The colonists hoped that the vessels would simply head back out to sea as others had been convinced to do in other ports, but the Collector of Customs refused to allow the ships to leave without payment of the taxes. To ensure that the ships did not return to England with their cargo, Hutchinson double-shotted the cannon at the British fort in the harbor and stationed two warships in the channel. Things were at a stalemate. On Saturday, December 16, eight days after the last ship had arrived in the harbor, the citizens of Boston gathered at Old South. **Josiah Quincy** recognized in the meeting attendants' outrage and the governor's intransigence the makings of a mighty tempest. "I see the clouds which now rise thick and fast upon the horizon," Quincy declared. "The thunders roll and the lightnings play, and to the God who rides on the whirlwind and directs the storm I commit my country!"

However, while British military leaders focused on this great assembly where Adams and Quincy were haranguing the crowd, other, much smaller meetings were taking place. One such meeting took place in the back rooms of a printing shop, where, availing themselves of a large bowl of potent fish house punch, Boston's **Sons of Liberty** transformed themselves into Mohawk Indians, complete with feathers, blankets, war paint, and tomahawks. John Adams noted later, however, "They were no ordinary Mohawks."

Early that evening, just as the meeting at Old South broke up, these "Mohawks" went on the warpath, leading the crowd to the bottom of Hutchinson Street, today's Pearl Street and to the harbor. Quickly and quietly, approximately 110 patriots boarded the ships, broke open tea cases, and flung them into the sea. In less than three hours, they had destroyed all 342 chests of tea. It is reported that perhaps 1,000 bystanders stood with mixed feelings and watched the protest. While many supported the Patriots' rebellious actions, some feared repercussions from the Crown. The Redcoats never appeared; the British guns never fired; the ships were not damaged; and no one was hurt. The Tea Party was a resounding success, but at what cost?

Myth or Truth? You Decide

It has been rumored and passed down through generations that some of the tea that was "tossed overboard" happened to land in the boats of a few waiting colonists. It is said that some long-time area families still do a tea ceremony each year, always using a bit of the stolen tea. Is there any truth to the story? You decide.

The next morning tons of soggy East India Company tea washed ashore. It was the beginning of the end for England in America. Boston and its "Mohawks" had successfully defied the Crown in an act that electrified the colonies and made independence seem possible. But Britain was not happy. The act of defiance would cost the colonists when England passed the Intolerable Acts a few months later and closed the port of Boston. Things were about to get worse.

The **Boston Tea Party Ships & Museum** has not had the best of luck. In 2001, the museum's gift shop was hit by lightning and was so extensively damaged that it was closed. In 2007 fire struck again, this time, reportedly started by a spark from nearby construction. The building was a total loss. However, Bostonians were not happy as the burned-out hulk of the building sat idle. Renovations promised by for-profit Historic Tours of America, the Florida-based company who leases the property from the city and also owns Old Town Trolley Tours, were reportedly being delayed by the ongoing construction on the Congress Street Bridge. Although the construction company in charge of the bridge repairs denies that the construction held things up, it hardly matters. Things were moving nowhere fast. Since then, however, Historic Tours of America has worked hard and poured hundreds of thousands of dollars into getting the site cleaned up and ready for an entirely new museum. They are in the process of building two new replica ships to add to the existing *Brig Beaver,* which has been in dry dock undergoing restoration since 2004. The ships are in Gloucester, Massachusetts where they are being revamped and built. If you want to watch, there's a live web cam on the company's website. These three ships will include interactive exhibits and provide visitors with an idea of how everything looked that rebellious December day. Historic Tours also promises that "museum spaces will be expanded to approximately twice their current size and will offer a multitude of easy to understand exhibits, video presentations, living history programs, and memorabilia that tell the story of the Boston Tea Party." Time will tell, but so far the new museum promises to be a remarkable stop once renovations are complete. To keep up to date with what is going on, visit www.bostonteapartyship.com.

OLD STATE HOUSE

206 Washington Street

The **Old State House,** built in 1713, is the oldest surviving public building in Boston. The building sits on the site of the original **Boston Town House,** a wooden structure built in 1657 and gifted to the town and its people by Boston merchant **Captain Robert Keayne.** Keayne's idea was to provide the town with a marketplace as well as a convenient meeting place. In 1711, the Town House was destroyed by fire and a proposal then launched to build a brick building to replace it. Four years later, the Old State House was built and became the gathering place for politics and debates.

In 1747, fire strikes again and portions of the interior of the Old State House and some of the brick walls are destroyed. What was rebuilt is what remains today. Portions of the original brick wall from 1713 also remain today. It is at this time that the **lion and unicorn** appear on the east side of the building.

Freedom Rings

Throughout the 1760s liberty's spokesmen used these halls to voice their opposition to British policy. Here **John Adams** and **John Hancock** inspired their peers. **Samuel Adams** encouraged colonists to oppose taxation without representation. And here **James Otis** delivered his impassioned, four-hour speech on the sanctity of individual rights, provoking John Adams to remark, "Then and there, the child Independence was born."

By 1774 the Massachusetts legislature had become a rebel congress that the Crown could not abide. **General Thomas Gage** was dispatched to Boston to replace **Thomas Hutchinson** as the new

The Old State House was almost dismantled and moved to Chicago until Bostonians rallied yet again to save a great piece of American history. PHOTO BY STEPHEN W. PIETRZYK

Massachusetts Bay Governor. No longer allowed to meet in the Old State House, members of the colonial legislature regrouped in **Salem.** Colonists were not happy with Britain's continued attempts to control them. In the fall of that year, the first **Continental Congress** met in Philadelphia. Strategies were discussed and a call to arms was heard. Minute Men companies started to form and the colonists prepared to fight. In 1775, battles took place at Lexington, Concord, and Bunker Hill as well as across New York. **George Washington** was named commander-in-chief of the newly formed **Continental Army.** One more attempt was made to reconcile with Britain, which she refused. The **Continental Navy** was formed to protect the coastline. Battles continued to rage as congress formally accepted the **Declaration of Independence,** which was read publicly for the first time from the balcony of the Old State House, now home, once again, to the colonial government. Years later, in 1780, **John Hancock** was inaugurated as

Massachusetts's first governor. The ceremony was held at the Old State House, which served as Massachusetts' State House until 1798 when the new State House was built on Beacon Hill.

Despite its stirring history, the Old State House fell on hard times. Once the new State House was built, the Old State House was renovated

Fun Facts

- As historic as the Old State House is, it has a modern purpose. In 1905, a subway station was opened in the building's basement and operates today as the **State Street Station** for the Red and Blue lines. Pretty convenient, huh?

- The British icons of the lion and unicorn originally adorned the building starting in 1747, after the first fire. However, sentiment against the Crown was so negative that they were torn down and burned in 1776. Those on the building today are replicas, which were placed there in 1882.

- State Street was formerly called **King's Street,** but was renamed in 1776.

- **William Lloyd Garrison** held some not-so-popular ideas as an abolitionist in 19th-century Boston. One night, after having spoken his mind one too many times, he was chased by a mob that meant to lynch him. He ran for cover to the Old State House, then the Boston City Hall, where he was later rescued and placed in the Leverett Street Jail for safekeeping.

and used as retail and restaurant space until 1830 at which time it was renovated once again and used as Boston City Hall for 10 years. In 1840, returned again to commercial use, the building started to fall into disrepair. In 1881 city fathers were undecided about its utility. Some, on learning the commercial value of the site, urged the building's demolition, whereupon the city of Chicago offered to purchase it for re-erection on the shores of Lake Michigan. The plan was so inimical to Bostonians that the historic edifice was immediately given a complete restoration. The Bostonian Society was founded to preserve the building.

Today, the Old State House is still cared for by The Bostonian Society as a museum and retains dignity amid the skyscrapers of the new Boston.

Old State House Information

Hours: Open daily 9 a.m. to 4 p.m. Jan; 9 a.m. to 5 p.m. Feb through June; 9 a.m. to 6 p.m. July and Aug. Closed New Year's Day, Thanksgiving, and Christmas. Closed the first workweek in Feb for annual maintenance.

Admission: Adults, $7.50; senior citizens and students over age 18, $6; children ages 6 to 18, $3; children 5 and younger and Bostonian Society members are admitted free

Phone: (617) 720-1713, ext. 21

Website: www.bostonhistory.org

Wheelchair accessibility: None, but be sure to check in before your trip, as the museum is working on this

---

Site of the Boston Massacre

Congress and State Streets

Tensions were escalating in the colonies. The Crown had sought to enforce one restrictive act after another, while Bostonians had persistently defied British authority. In an attempt to maintain order and obedience, and to enforce her rule, Great Britain sent troops to Boston in 1768. However, the presence of the **Redcoats** only served to spur the colonists, including the **Sons of Liberty** to greater resistance. By 1770 Bostonians were openly clashing with the Redcoats; fistfights and angry confrontations were not uncommon. The colonists were doing everything in their power to weaken the British troops, including trying to get the soldiers to desert the army, and printing propaganda (or was it?) of horrible acts the soldiers were committing against the people of Boston. Things were getting dicey.

On the evening of March 5, conflict hit a fever pitch. While there are many versions of the story and details vary from one to the other, we did our best to put together how things might have happened. That evening, around 7 or 8 p.m., a young wigmaker's apprentice named **Edward Garrick** arrived at the Customs House and said something insulting to British **Captain John Goldfinch. Private Hugh White** was on duty outside and would not abide young Garrick's disrespect of his commanding officer. He reportedly stepped forward and struck young Garrick on the side of the head. Garrick's friend, **Bartholomew Broaders** stepped forward and hurled a few insults of his own. Then a crowd began to gather and the British soldiers were quickly outnumbered.

British **Captain Thomas Preston** was well aware of the rising discontent and was told that night that Bostonians were assembling to attack the troops. Upon heading to the main guard, Preston reported utter confusion. "In a few minutes," Preston wrote of that day, "about a hundred people passed and went toward the custom-house, where the King's money is lodged. They immediately surrounded the sentinel posted there, and with clubs and other weapons threatened to execute their vengeance on him. A townsman assured me he heard the mob declare they would murder him. I fearing their plundering the King's chest, immediately sent a non-commissioned officer and twelve men to protect both the sentinel and the King's money, and very soon followed myself, to prevent disorder. . . . So far was I from intending death, that the troops went to the spot where the unhappy affair took place, without loading their pieces."

Things were about to get worse, however. The growing and increasingly agitated colonists were calling out, "Come out, you rascals, you bloody-backs, you lobster scoundrels—fire if you dare. God damn you, fire and be damned!"

No longer in the middle of traffic, this ring of cobblestones has been reassembled in a newer, more prominent memorial at the same location, but now embedded in the sidewalk. PHOTO BY STEPHEN W. PIETRZYK

The British soldiers stood their ground as the crowd closed in on them, pointing bayonets and sticks. Suddenly, a British Private named **Hugh Montgomery** was hit with a stick and instantly fired into the crowd. Before Preston could yell a reprimand and stop the shot, he, too, was hit with a stick. The crowd continued throwing snowballs and sticks. The scene was chaos. Control was lost and Preston reports someone yelling, "Damn your bloods, why don't you fire?" and that was all they needed. The British soldiers discharged their muskets point-blank at their tormentors.

The mob scattered. But three men lay dead, including **Crispus Attucks, Samuel Gray,** and 17-year-old **James Caldwell.** Of the eight wounded the townsfolk carried away that night, two later died of their injuries, including 17-year-old **Samuel Maverick** who died the next day and **Patrick Carr,** an Irish immigrant and leather worker who died two weeks later. Preston maintained that it had not been planned, that he had not been the one to yell "Fire," which had possibly been mistaken as an order.

A Sixth Victim?
While historical accounts claim that there were five victims of the Boston Massacre, there is possibly a sixth. Young **Christopher Monk** was also shot that fateful day. Accounts indicate that he was mortally wounded when a shot entered his body above his groin and exited out his hip. His injuries were so severe that Monk was disabled for the rest of his life. He died 10 years later at the age of 27, and many say the wound he received on March 5, 1770, most likely contributed to his early death.

The Sons of Liberty wasted no time spinning the incident to their advantage. **Sam Adams** held funerals for the victims and insisted they be buried in his family tomb in **Granary Burying Ground,**

Where There's a Will . . .

The story goes that one evening, **Dr. Joseph Warren,** a handsome, aristocratic physician, was prevented from entering the **Old South Meeting House.** Not to be deterred, the young rebel climbed over the heads of British soldiers, through a second-story window in back, and addressed the patriots inside. His daring so humiliated the troops that he became a marked man, but he didn't stop there. On March 6, 1775, Dr. Warren, known for his eloquent speech, was chosen to deliver the oration on the fifth anniversary of the **Boston Massacre.** Held purposefully at the Old South Meeting House, these speeches were held annually as a way to encourage anti-Britain feelings across the colonies. Dr. Warren was in his glory. It was noted that even the British soldiers in attendance were captivated, until the end when tensions got a little heated. Things were kept under control, however, and the oration ended without incident. Dr. Warren continued his role in the revolution by sending Paul Revere, along with William Dawes, on the midnight ride one month later to inform Samuel Adams and John Hancock that the "Regulars were out." Two months after that, Dr. Warren would lose his life after valiantly fighting at the **Battle of Bunker Hill** in 1775. It is said that both Generals Putnam and Prescott offered to give up their leadership and instead take orders from Warren. The unassuming doctor refused, saying he was there to learn from them. He was killed in the third assault on the hill. From young rebel to avid Revolutionary, Dr. Joseph Warren made his mark in history.

solidifying their reputations as martyrs. **Paul Revere** created a now famous engraving that showed the British soldiers firing on the crowd, along with several other inaccuracies, and furthered anti-British sentiment. Prints of the engraving along with news of the event spread quickly throughout the countryside, fueling the fires that already burned.

The British soldiers and Captain Preston were brought to trial months later for their involvement in the incident. **John Adams** and

Josiah Quincy, among others, defended the men. Though all but two were acquitted of manslaughter, the Boston Massacre ever afterward served as a rallying point for the patriot cause.

Until recently, a simple ring of cobblestones in the middle of Congress and State Streets marked the spot of the altercation that day. However, safety was a concern, as getting to the exact spot to view the memorial was a bit tricky—it being in the middle of a traffic island and all. In May 2011, MBTA removed the ring of cobblestones, and they were safely stored by the National Park Service while the intersection was being upgraded. Plans are to enlarge the sidewalk in order to encompass the memorial, which will now be surrounded by a bronze ring to give it the prominence it deserves.

FANEUIL HALL

Dock Square

In 1742, New York–born merchant **Peter Faneuil** presented his adopted community of Boston with a proposal for a central market building as a remedy for the "disadvantage under which trade was conducted with no market house as a center of exchange." A petition was drafted and presented to the selectmen, who called a town meeting to discuss the idea. Many people turned out to vote on Faneuil's proposal and he was almost turned down, as many had been before him. In order to save the idea and appease the detractors, the following line was added to the proposal: ". . . and we would humbly propose that, notwithstanding the said building should be encouraged and come to effect, yet that the market people should be at liberty to carry their marketing wheresoever they please about the town to dispose of it."

The Jolly Bachelor

Peter Faneuil was no sober-sided businessman. He inherited most of his money from his uncle Andrew after promising that he would never marry. He honored the promise and enjoyed a reputation as **"the Jolly Bachelor of Boston."** He even christened one of his ships the *Jolly Bachelor.*

Sadly, the first major public use of Faneuil's town hall was a memorial for Faneuil himself, who died in 1743, only months after the building was completed. John Lovell, Sr., then headmaster of the Boston Latin School presented the eulogy. In contrast to the saucy sobriquet of his bachelor days, Faneuil, son of a French Huguenot refugee, was remembered in his obituary as "the most public spirited man . . . that ever yet appeared on the northern continent of America." Peter Faneuil is buried in the Granary Burying Ground.

This worked and an agreement was reached. The project was given the go-ahead. When the building was completed in 1742, the townspeople were impressed that Faneuil had gone above and beyond his original proposal, he had not only built a marketplace, but "also superadded a spacious and most beautiful town hall over it, and several other convenient rooms, which may prove very beneficial to the town."

For many years the handsome redbrick building welcomed trading ships into a port bustling with business. The first-floor marketplace offered vegetables, fish, and other merchandise in a centralized location. In the years leading up to the Revolutionary War, the second-story town hall reverberated with tumultuous meetings and midnight assemblies. It is said that the building gained its nickname the **"Cradle of Liberty,"** because the voices of the people were heard there. Boston's orators thundered their dissent from the Navigation Acts, the

The famous grasshopper weathervane atop Faneuil Hall was once a test to see if a person was friend or foe. PHOTO BY STEPHEN W. PIETRZYK

Intolerable Acts, and all other acts of the Crown that would restrict the traditional rights and privileges of New England. Here the citizens of the New World claimed the rights of free men.

Odd Man Out

Five men from Massachusetts signed The Declaration of Independence, but only four are depicted in the artwork at Faneuil Hall. Who's missing? **Elbridge Gerry.**

After a fire destroyed the interior of the building in 1761, it was rebuilt within two years using public funding. In 1806 **Charles Bulfinch** enlarged and modified the building, doubling the size of the original structure but retaining and repeating the Doric pilasters and arched windows of portrait painter John Smibert's original design. He also added a spacious third story and repositioned the cupola.

When you visit Faneuil Hall, be sure to take note of the **famous weathervane** created by Shem Drowne atop the cupola. Peter Faneuil himself is said to have chosen the gilded grasshopper with the green glass eye to crown his gift to the city. He most likely borrowed the symbol of finance from London where Martin's Bank and the Royal Exchange were also topped by grasshopper vanes. The grasshopper became so strongly associated with Boston, that an American consul once tested citizens claiming to be residents of the city by asking them to identify the most renowned weathervane in the United States. If they failed the question, they were suspect.

Listen a Spell

Historical talks are given at Faneuil Hall daily every half hour on the half hour, 9:30 a.m. to 4:30 p.m., except when the hall is being used for special events.

In 1825, Bostonians decided that more market space was needed downtown. The old Town Dock area was filled in and the three granite market buildings known as **Quincy Market** were built. These buildings, along with Faneuil Hall continue as a marketplace to this day. So, even though she no longer welcomes ships in the harbor, Faneuil Hall still serves as a handsome mercantile landmark with more than 250 years of history.

Today, the ground floor houses retail and eating establishments. The second floor remains as a meeting hall. It is staffed by knowledgeable National Park Service rangers and is open to visitors throughout the year. The top floor of the building houses a **museum of the Ancient and Honorable Artillery Company of Massachusetts,** which has occupied space in the hall since 1746. Maintained jointly by the City of Boston and the National Park Service, Faneuil Hall is the centerpiece of a scene fully as busy and as colorful as in the days of merchant shipping and revolutionary zeal.

Side Trip: Quincy Market

In 1823, one year after Boston became a city, **Josiah Quincy** (1772–1864), who had served Massachusetts as a congressman in Washington, was elected mayor for the first of what would be five terms.

The dynamic Quincy, later president of **Harvard College,** greatly improved municipal services. During his tenure he established a standard of service for cities everywhere. He instituted a system for cleaning streets, improved education, and reorganized the police force and fire department. Then he turned his attention to improving and enlarging Boston's limited market facilities "without great expense to the city."

Braving widespread doubt and criticism, the resourceful mayor ordered a landfill of the stagnant waters near the Town Dock. Where wharf rats had scurried, there arose a central marketplace designed by the progressive Boston architect **Alexander Parris.** The huge two-story building (50 by 535 feet), with its Greek porticoes and domed central pavilion, was constructed in 1825 of granite from the quarries of **Quincy,** Massachusetts.

The project took one year, and sale of the newly created real estate paid for the entire project. Moreover, the brick warehouses that flanked the market and other structures that were built on the six new streets increased the tax base and filled the city's coffers.

The area fell on hard times in the mid-1900s and many of the buildings stood vacant and dilapidated. A major renovation and renewal in the 1970s brought life back to the marketplace. Today **Quincy Market,**

Made up of four buildings—Faneuil Hall, Quincy Market, North Market, and South Market, Faneuil Hall marketplace offers myriad shopping and eating opportunities. PHOTO BY STEPHEN W. PIETRZYK

redeveloped by **James Rouse,** constitutes one of the finest urban shopping and dining areas in the world. It serves as an inspiration to old cities everywhere that aspire to revive their downtown areas. Also known as **Faneuil Hall Marketplace,** it is made up of 4 buildings—Faneuil Hall, Quincy Market, North Market, and South Market. Together, they boast more than 100 retail stores and individual pushcarts, more than 40 eateries, and 17 restaurants, including the replica of famous **Cheers** where, I've got to say it, everyone knows your name (the original is on Beacon Hill). Quincy Market has been so successful that it is one of the most

---

I Have to Go Where?

When taking the T to Quincy Market, remember to take the Green/Blue Line to the Government Center. Do not get confused with the "Quincy" T stops on the Red Line. Those stops are in the city of Quincy, just south of Boston, not Quincy Market.

---

visited attractions in Boston, so much so, that many locals suggest you steer clear of it! But we say it's worth a stop at least. While some of the stores are your run-of-the-mill stores that you'll find in any mall across the country, there are some neat finds to be discovered. Boston memorabilia abounds as does Harvard wear and other unique treasures. If you keep in mind the time of day you arrive there, you may be able to avoid slightly horrendous crowds. On nice days, you'll be treated to street performers throughout the quaintly cobblestoned plaza. You're likely to see everything from clowns to magicians, musicians to jugglers, and even some great reenactments! There are also seasonal events such as the 4th of July Harborfest, the annual tree lighting, and a summer concert series, as well as numerous in-store and in-restaurant events.

Quincy Market Information

Hours: 10 a.m. to 7 p.m. Mon through Thurs; 10 a.m. to 9 p.m. Fri and Sat; noon to 6 p.m. Sun, Jan 2 through mid-Feb; 10 a.m. to 9 p.m. Mon through Sat; noon to 6 p.m. Sun, mid-Feb through Jan 1. Extended hours for the food colonnade

Admission: Free

Phone: (617) 338-2323

Website: www.faneuilhallmarketplace.com

Wheelchair accessibility: Yes, but be aware that surrounding areas are cobblestoned and can be a bit tricky to navigate

---

Pit Stop: Union Oyster House

Established in 1826, the **Union Oyster House** (41 Union St.) is America's oldest restaurant in continuous service. The building has been standing for more than 250 years and is so old that no one knows when it was actually built or who built it! Records do show, however, that the building served as a dress goods business; a print shop where *The*

Massachusetts Spy was published; a silk and dry goods store; an official pay station for Federal troops; and a home to Louis Philippe, future king of France. In 1826, the **Oyster Bar** was installed and many historical notables were frequent customers, including Daniel Webster.

This wonderful building is so full of history that it's a must-see on the Freedom Trail. Be sure to check out **John F. Kennedy's booth** upstairs and learn about all the other famous people who have graced the restaurant's rooms.

While weekends can be busy, weekdays are a bit more manageable. If you can time your walk right, it's a great place to stop for lunch or dinner. If not, why not just stop in for a specialty Sam Adams beer that's brewed special for the restaurant? To make a reservation or for more information, visit www.unionoysterhouse.com.

Side Trip: New England Holocaust Memorial

They came first for the Communists,
and I didn't speak up because I wasn't a Communist.

Then they came for the Jews,
and I didn't speak up because I wasn't a Jew.

Then they came for the trade unionists,
and I didn't speak up because I wasn't a trade
unionist.

Then they came for the Catholics,
and I didn't speak up because I was a Protestant.

Then they came for me,
and by that time no one was left to speak up.

—Martin Niemöller (1892–1984)

Martin Niemöller (1892–1984) was an outspoken pastor of Protestant faith who spent seven years in a German concentration camp. While numerous versions of the above quote exist, the sentiment is the same in them all. We must stand up for ourselves and our neighbors. If we don't, those who thirst for power will rule. It was a sentiment our founding fathers understood well. And, as much as the Freedom Trail is a tribute to the bravery of the actions behind that understanding, the **New England Holocaust Memorial** is a testament to what happens when patriots do not or cannot act. This memorial stands in stark contrast between what freedom from oppression can achieve and what happens when that freedom does not and cannot exist.

Designed by **Stanley Saitowitz** and completed in 1995, the New England Holocaust Memorial gleams at a location between Congress and Union Streets near **Faneuil Hall**. Its **six, 54-foot glass towers** are said to shimmer during the day and glow at night. There is one tower for each of the six death camps, and upon these towers are 6 million etched numbers representing the registration numbers of the 6 million souls who perished in those camps. Steam from 6-foot square pits in the ground at the base of each tower rises through these chambers. If you peer into these pits, you will see coals smoldering at the bottom, and if you look carefully, you will see the flickering light from the coals illuminate the name of the death camp that the tower represents, which is also etched into the bottom of the tower. If you're noticing the prominence of the number 6, good, it's not a mistake. It is also said to represent the six memorial candles on a menorah.

As you wander the black granite path that meanders through the towers, take note of the word REMEMBER carved in English and Hebrew on one end of the pathway and Yiddish and English at the other end, and remember how important it is to stand for each other against evil.

Also along the path are haunting quotes from Holocaust survivors and facts about this time in history. Some tell of their time in the camps, while others tell tales of survival and hope.

While this memorial is a step off the Freedom Trail, it's well worth the visit. For more information, visit www.nehm.org or call (617) 457-8755.

Pit Stop: Haymarket Square

If you happen to be in Boston on a Friday or Saturday, don't leave without experiencing **Haymarket,** Boston's historic open-air market. It is said that vendors have been selling their wares in this location since 1830! Some of the stands you'll find here have been run by the same North End family for generations. Incredible deals are to be found on produce at most any time of the year. As you wander through the chaos on Blackstone Street (between North and Hanover Streets), you'll hear shouts of "Strawberries, one dollar! Cukes, three for two dollars! Get 'em while they're fresh!" Keep in mind that the market is open from dawn to dusk, so if you have miles to cover on the Trail, time this strategically. Maybe pick up some fruit to go with a pastry from the North End on

If you happen to be in Boston on a Friday or Saturday, don't leave without experiencing Haymarket, Boston's historic open-air market. PHOTO BY STEPHEN W. PIETRZYK

Boston's Historic North End is home to wonderful eateries, the Paul Revere House, Old North Church, and other fascinating historic stops. PHOTO BY STEPHEN W. PIETRZYK

your way to Charlestown, or pack some fresh veggies for the ride home after a day of walking the Trail. You can also pick up local seafood, but if you're traveling a ways it might not be the best idea. I've also seen cheese and bread offered, but have never tried it. You really can't beat the prices, but keep in mind that most of this produce comes from wholesale markets inventory that needed to be cleared for the weekend. While it's mostly fresh, don't plan on it staying fresh for days—if you're going to eat it that weekend, great, but if you need something to last for a week or so, beware. It's always a good idea, too, to have some $1 bills on hand so the vendors don't have to make change.

PAUL REVERE HOUSE

19 North Square

The oldest building in downtown Boston, the **Paul Revere House** sits on what was originally the site of the parsonage of the famous **Increase Mather,** autocratic minister of the first **Old North Meeting House** and father to diarist and witch-hunter the **Reverend Cotton Mather.** The Mather family lived in a house at this site until 1676 when their home was destroyed by a devastating fire along with about 45 other buildings.

The Old North congregation built the current structure on the site around 1680, which they sold a year later to merchant **Robert Howard.** This new house, typical of 17th-century Massachusetts architecture, was built in the English Tudor style, with a steep pitched roof; a front overhang with ornamental drops; and at the attic level, a single or double gable facing the street; casement windows with diamond-shaped panes; massive end chimneys; and a simple floor plan without interior hallways.

By contemporary standards the house was unusually spacious, having two large rooms in the front and two more in an ell that extended back toward the garden. The whole structure was framed in heavy carved timbers held together by wooden pegs.

Here Robert Howard and his successors dwelled one block from the sea, overlooking triangular North Square with its market, guardhouse, meetinghouse, and pump—a veritable beehive of activity and one of the town's most fashionable neighborhoods.

It was still a prime location in 1770, when **Paul Revere** purchased the Howard house and moved in with his family. By this time, the house had been modernized considerably. A partial third story with a row of windows had replaced the front gables, and new sash windows had

The oldest building in downtown Boston, this house was home to the Revere family from 1770 until 1800. PHOTO BY STEPHEN W. PIETRZYK

replaced the casement windows. Inside the heavy beams had been cased in the front rooms and wainscoting and raised moldings added.

Revere, the son of a Huguenot, a Protestant refugee from France named **Apollos Rivoire,** was the talented possessor of a wide variety

Crowded Quarters

While Paul Revere had sixteen children (eight with each of his wives), they never all lived under one roof together. In fact, his oldest and his youngest were thirty years apart. Moreover, while sixteen sounds like a lot, it was not unheard of in the times. Due to the high childhood mortality rate, many of these children never grew to adulthood. In fact, five of Revere's children died before the age of five. At the time that the Reveres would have lived at the North Square house, the family had between five and nine children living with them.

of skills and of industry enough to make good use of them. The proprietor of a Clark's Wharf shop in which he fashioned objects of gold and silver, Revere was also a designer/engraver of copperplate, a dentist of sorts, engraver and printer of the Commonwealth's paper money, a Son of Liberty and prominent rebel organizer, and an excellent horseman entrusted with many important messages prior to the Revolution. In the age before specialization, he was one of Boston's preeminent generalists.

The Famous Midnight Ride

Paul Revere is undoubtedly best known for his midnight ride to Lexington to warn local Sons of Liberty John Hancock and Samuel Adams that British troops were planning to cross the Charles River into Charlestown and then march to Lexington to arrest them. It was the year 1775 and Revere was employed as an express messenger and was often entrusted with important information. On the night in question, Dr. Joseph Warren sent for Revere and William Dawes to have them deliver the news by separate routes. Revere then had to cross the Charles and borrow a horse to make his way into Lexington, while Dawes traveled on land the entire way. Once there, the two decided to continue on to Concord, where weapons and supplies were stored, to sound the warning. They were joined by Dr. Samuel Prescott. On their way to Concord, however, the three were stopped by a British patrol. Prescott made an immediate escape with Dawes soon after him. Revere was held for a bit before being released and returning to Lexington. Prescott was the only one to actually make it to Concord to deliver the warning. Dawes was forced to retreat to Lexington instead of continuing to Concord.

It was this same night that the signal of two lanterns were hung in the Old North Church to alert the Sons of Liberty in Charlestown that the troops were leaving Boston "by sea" (actually by river) as opposed to land. As the poem goes: "One if by land, two if by sea, and I on the opposite shore will be . . ." Revere had arranged the signal in case he was unable to make it out of Boston to deliver the warning himself.

Today Revere is remembered for his midnight ride rather than for his bills and bells and bowls. The galloping rhythms and stirring language of Henry Wadsworth Longfellow's ballad, published in 1861, made Paul Revere one of the most celebrated heroes of the American Revolution.

After the Revolution Revere settled down to a life of hard and rewarding work as one of the nation's first industrialists, developing his bell and cannon foundry and copper works into important Boston enterprises. In the 1790s, Revere also served as Grand Master of the Massachusetts Grand Lodge of Masons, as president of the Boston Board of Health, as Suffolk County Coroner, and helped found the Massachusetts Charitable Mechanics Association, one of the earliest benevolent societies for the working class.

Revere sold his house in 1800, when he moved to more elegant quarters, but the three-story North Square building remained associated with his memory and was preserved through many years of neighborhood demolition and renewal.

For Whom the Bell Tolls
Be sure to stop in **The Paul Revere House Courtyard** to see the 900-pound bell manufactured by Paul Revere & Sons. There are also a small Revere-made mortar and bolt from USS *Constitution.*

The **Paul Revere Memorial Association** acquired the house in 1907 after Paul Revere's great grandson **John P. Reynolds, Jr.,** purchased the property to ensure it wasn't demolished. The Association took two years to restore the building to its colonial appearance. They removed the third-story addition and a small two-story addition at the back, returning the exterior of the building to approximately its 1680 appearance. The Association was able to keep close to 90 percent of the original structure, as well as two doors, three window frames, and portions of the flooring, foundation, inner wall material, and raftering; that's quite a save! While three of the rooms have been restored to showcase what they might have looked like in Revere's days, one—the ground floor front room—has been restored and furnished to reflect the era of Robert Howard. The museum always has Revere silver and a number of pieces of Revere furniture on display, plus changing exhibits that include Revere documents, engravings, and other memorabilia.

Paul Revere lived to be 83 years old. He retired from the copper business in 1811 at the age of 76. His wife Rachel and son Paul died in 1813. Revere himself left this world on May 10, 1818, of natural causes and is buried in Granary Burying Ground.

The Paul Revere House Information

Hours: 9:30 a.m. to 5:15 p.m. daily, Apr 15 through Oct 31; 9:30 a.m. to 4:15 p.m. daily, Nov 1 through Apr 14 (except closed Mon, Jan through Mar); closed Thanksgiving, Christmas, and New Year's Day

Admission: Adults, $3.50; seniors and college students, $3; ages 5 to 17, $1. Children under 5 and North End residents are admitted free at all times. Patriots' Passes purchased online or at Old South accepted.

Phone: (617) 523-2338

Website: www.paulreverehouse.org

Wheelchair accessibility: Courtyard, first floor, and program area. Visit the website for more detailed information.

Pit Stop: Modern Pastry & Mike's Pastry

As you enter the **North End,** you will undoubtedly see people walking around with pastry boxes. Chances are they will be from either Mike's Pastry or Modern Pastry. You really can't go wrong with either one. The only drawback is that you most likely have to wait in a bit of a line to get something. The lines move quickly, though, and afford you time to make your choices! Whether you're wanting a jumbo chocolate-chip cookie, a delicious cannoli, or some other sumptuous dessert, hop in line and prepare your taste buds!

Modern Pastry is located at 257 Hanover St, and is open Sun to Thurs 8 a.m. to 10 p.m., Fri 8 a.m. to 11 p.m., and Sat 8 a.m. to midnight.

Mike's Pastry is located at 300 Hanover St. and is open daily at 8 a.m. It closes at 10 p.m. Sun, Mon, and Tues, 10:30 p.m. Wed and Thurs, and 11:30 p.m. Fri and Sat.

Side Trip: Saint Stephen's Church

401 Hanover St., Facing Paul Revere Mall

Saint Stephen's Church, originally the **New North Congregational Church,** is the only house of worship designed by **Charles Bulfinch** that is still standing in Boston. The church features a pilastered facade in what has been described as a "bold and commanding style," surmounted by a clock tower, a belfry, and an Eastern dome. Bulfinch relieved the front elevation with a Palladian window, a lunette above, and his characteristic graceful blind-arch windows.

Bulfinch's church cost $26,570 to build. The cornerstone was laid on September 23, 1802, and the building dedicated on May 2, 1804. The following year the congregation purchased a bell from the foundry of Paul Revere.

The congregation already had a long history before it acquired the building. In 1714 seventeen successful Boston artisans had banded together to form the **Second Congregational Society** that, they said, would provide spiritual sustenance to the city's "humble" citizens. "Unassisted by the more wealthy part of the community except by their prayers and good wishes," the artisans erected the **New North Church building,** a small wooden meetinghouse.

The copper-covered dome of Saint Stephen's was discovered during a restoration project in 1862. The copper was originally supplied by Paul Revere. PHOTO BY STEPHEN W. PIETRZYK

Under the **Reverend John Webb,** the society prospered. But in 1719, with the introduction of the **Reverend Peter Thatcher** as Webb's colleague, a bitter and messy division developed within the group. As a result a group broke away to found the **New Brick North Church.** They topped their new house of worship with a rooster weathervane, also known as a weathercock, designed by **Shem Drowne** of Faneuil Hall grasshopper fame. According to local legend, the weathervane was barely installed on its perch when a gust of wind turned the cockerel's head in the direction of New North. A bystander, aware that the cock is a symbol of the Apostle Peter's betrayal and that Reverend Thatcher's first name was Peter, derisively crowed three times in the direction of New North. The New Brick was therefore also called **"Revenge Church"** and the **"Cockerel Church."** The weathervane was taken down and eventually found a perch on the spire of First Church in Cambridge, Congregational, where it can be seen today.

In 1730 New North was enlarged. The congregation continued to grow even still, and after the Revolution required a larger home. In 1802, the old wooden New North was razed, and in its place rose a new **brick New North** (not to be confused with the New Brick North Church), using some of the old building's timbers.

Like many other congregations in the early part of the 19th century, New North's adopted Unitarianism. In 1814, the church was renamed the **Second Church, Unitarian.** As early as the 1820s, however, the North End was changing, and by the 1850s the area had become solidly Irish Catholic. In 1862 **Father John J. Williams,** administrator at the time and later archbishop of Boston, purchased the church and dedicated it to **Saint Stephen,** the first Christian martyr. By 1900, however, the Irish of the North End were replaced by the Italians, whose descendants continue to worship here.

Saint Stephen's Church Information

Hours: Open daily, Mass is held Sun at 11 a.m., Tues through Fri at 7:30 a.m., and Sat at 4:30 p.m.

Admission: Free

Phone: (617) 523-1230

Wheelchair accessibility: No

Side Trip: Paul Revere Mall

Hanover Street, Next to the Old North Church

Paul Revere Mall, the small park linking **Christ Church ("Old North")** and **Saint Stephen's Church,** is dominated by **Cyrus Dallin**'s equestrian statue of that celebrated midnight rider, **Paul Revere.** Thirteen bronze plaques set in the mall's walls recount the role that the **North End** and its people played in the history of Boston from 1630 to 1918.

One of the North End's most famous residents, Paul Revere is well known for his famous ride from Boston to Lexington on April 18, 1775, to bring the latest intelligence about the British to John Hancock and Samuel Adams. General Thomas Gage and his troops were preparing to march out and capture the colonial militia's contraband muskets, gunpowder, and cannons stored in Concord. No one knew, however, when the British troops would march or the route they would take. Once it was learned that they would be crossing the water, two lanterns were

Paul Revere rides tall with the steeple of the Old North Church in the background. PHOTO BY STEPHEN W. PIETRZYK

hung at Old North and Revere and William Dawes set out to deliver the news in person.

Revere thundered past sleeping farms, dismounting and pounding on doors at every village common or knot of country homes. Behind him he left bells ringing and men shouting and dogs barking. Minutemen poured out of their homes to form ranks against the enemy. Other horsemen saddled up and rode off to spread the word. By the time Revere reached Lexington, the whole countryside was up in arms.

It's a common misconception that Paul Revere called out "The British are coming!" on his midnight ride. In fact, the colonists *were* British, so if he had yelled those words, one can imagine many of them wondering, "The British are coming? Where are we going?" It has also been said perhaps he yelled, "The Redcoats are coming!" or maybe "The Lobsterbacks are coming!" The truth is, what he most likely said was "The Regulars are out." Sam Adams and John Hancock would have known just who he was talking about. Not as exciting, but the truth nonetheless.

While incredibly important and fun to talk about, Revere was not the only North Ender to contribute to the cause. Be sure to stroll through the mall and check out the plaques to learn about the others before heading on to the Old North Church.

OLD NORTH CHURCH

193 Salem Street

The building we know today as **Old North Church,** also called **Christ Church,** opened its doors to worshippers on December 29, 1723; it is the oldest house of worship still standing in Boston. This was actually the second Episcopal church in Boston—the first is **King's Chapel**—and is generally thought to have been designed by the Boston print-seller **William Price** in the manner of **Sir Christopher Wren**'s London churches. The original brick tower was surmounted by one of the architectural wonders of Old Boston, a magnificent spire soaring 191 feet above the street.

It may have soared a bit too far, however, because it came crashing down in a hurricane in the fall of 1804. **Charles Bulfinch,** carefully preserving its "symmetry and proportions," provided a new steeple that was a bit shorter. The Bulfinch steeple fell victim to Hurricane Carol in 1954. The present steeple, a reproduction of the first, is capped with **Shem Drowne**'s original 1740 weathervane, a swallowtail banner with a ball and star above. Drowne was also the maker of the famous grasshopper weathervane that sits atop Faneuil Hall. He is buried at Copp's Hill Burying Ground.

What's in a Name?
This is not Boston's first Old North Church. The old Old North Meeting House, built in 1650 in North Square, was destroyed by fire in 1676, was rebuilt, and stood for another hundred years before the British troops tore it down for firewood. There was no confusion, however, because at the time the two churches coexisted, the one on Salem Street was known as Christ Church.

This lovely old church, once a bastion of Loyalist support for the British Empire, is a well known landmark of the Revolutionary era thanks to Henry Wadsworth Longfellow's poem **"Paul Revere's Ride."** The famous lantern signals, displayed in this church's steeple on the night of April 18, 1775, were at the heart of a back-up plan created by Paul Revere to warn fellow patriots of the departure of British Regulars for the towns of Lexington and Concord lest he be captured as he tried to leave Boston. Revere put the first part of this plan into motion in a meeting with colonial militia from Charlestown just days before the night of April 18. He told the militiamen to keep a constant watch on the top window of the Old North steeple. One lantern meant that the troops were going by land across Boston Neck, while two meant they would be ferried across the Charles River by boat. Eighty years later, Longfellow would immortalize this plan with the phrase "One if by land, two if by sea."

Revere put the second part of his plan in motion with patriot members of the Old North congregation in that same week before April 18. That much is known from Revere's own account of that night's events. But his account is not specific about whom he asked to hang the lanterns, and as a result there is some debate. There are two men who have been given credit over the years, Robert Newman, the sexton of the church, and Captain John Pulling Jr., a member of the church vestry and of the Sons of Liberty. Both would have had access to the church and both were Patriots.

At this point, the story of the lanterns becomes a tale based more on historical speculation and imagination than on fact. Whoever the man or men were, they used the keys to open the doors that visitors still enter today, entered the church locking the doors behind them, and left one or more of their fellow patriots outside to keep watch. Then they took one of the two staircases at the back of the church to a door behind the organ where they then climbed a series of ladders eight stories up the interior of the steeple. When they reached the top, they lit two lanterns with flint and steel and held them out the window for just under a minute, signifying that the British would be going by river. When Paul Revere arrived in Charlestown on that night after successfully sneaking out of Boston undetected, the militiamen waiting for him there told him that they had seen his signal from the church. The word was out, and the next day would bring the battles of Lexington and Concord.

Old North Church is the oldest house of worship still standing in Boston and is the site of the famous lantern hanging the night of Paul Revere's ride. PHOTO BY SHUTTERSTOCK

The interior of the church is just as beautiful as the outside. Many of the interior fittings were donated by philanthropic Englishmen interested in propagating the doctrines of the Church of England in Puritan Boston. **King George II** himself donated several pieces of the silver communion service, which are now on display at the Museum of Fine Arts. **Captain William Maxwell** donated the brass chandeliers to the church in 1724. These chandeliers still hang today and are lit on special occasions. They are the only source of light on the first floor of the church. In 1746, **Captain Thomas Gruchy,** commander of the privateer *Queen of Hungary,* presented the four trumpeting angels that grace the choir loft, booty from a French vessel.

The pews with high walls (to keep the parishoners warm) bear brass plates with names of Revolutionary-era families, some of whose descendants may still worship here. Be sure to check out pews 54 and 29. The bust of George Washington at the front of the church is a fine likeness of the president, according to the Marquis de Lafayette.

Do You Dare?

If you're game, be sure to ask about the half-hour Behind the Scenes tour offered by the Old North Foundation whereby you can visit the **church's crypt** and **climb to the bell ringing tower.** Used between 1732 and 1860, the crypt contains thirty-seven tombs that contain approximately 1,100 bodies. Those buried include Timothy Cutler, the church's first rector; British Marine Major John Pitcairn, who died at the Battle of Bunker Hill; many soldiers from the Battle of Bunker Hill, and Captain Samuel Nicholson, the first captain of USS *Constitution.* In the bell ringing chamber is the control center for the change bells. Fifteen-year-old Paul Revere was a founding member of the first guild of bell ringers there in 1750. The tour promises to be fascinating as you learn how the tombs were built and about the 270-year history of the famous Old North steeple.

The church also boasts what is said to be the **oldest set of change bells in North America.** The set of eight bells were cast by Abell Rudhall in Gloucester, England in 1744 and hung a year later. Each of the bells is inscribed with a sentiment, including "We are the first ring of bells cast for the British Empire in North America," "Since generosity has opened our mouths, our tongues shall ring aloud its praise," and, of course, "God preserve the Church of England." Today the bells are maintained and rung regularly by the Massachusetts Institute of Technology Guild of Bellringers. More information can be found at their website http://bellringers.scripts.mit.edu/www/change-ringing/in-new-england/old-north-church.

After more than two centuries, Old North Church is still an active Episcopal congregation, with services on Thursday evenings and Sunday mornings.

Old North Church Information

Hours: Jan and Feb, 10 a.m. to 4 p.m. Tues through Sun, closed Mon; Mar through May, 9 a.m. to 5 p.m. daily; June through Oct, 9 a.m. to 6 p.m. daily; Nov and Dec, 10 a.m. to 5 p.m. daily. Closed to visitors Thanksgiving and Christmas. Sunday services are held at 9 a.m. and 11 a.m., Thursday service at 6 p.m.

Admission: Free, but a donation is appreciated

Phone: (617) 523-6676

Website: www.oldnorth.org

Wheelchair accessibility: Yes

COPP'S HILL BURIAL GROUND

Hull and Snowhill Streets

Copp's Hill Burial Ground in the North End was established in 1659 and is Boston's second-oldest cemetery, the first being King's Chapel Burying Ground. The area, originally called Windmill Hill for the large wind-powered grinding mill that used to occupy the slope, now takes its name from its former owner and Boston cobbler **William Copp.**

Although now a peaceful resting place, the hill's strategic location served in the Revolutionary War. By that time, several shipyards and wharves had been established at the base of Copp's Hill. Like Beacon Hill, Copp's Hill was once a good deal higher; its crest commanded an excellent view of Boston and, across the Charles River, of Charlestown. Here in 1775, shortly after the battles at Lexington and Concord, the British set up a battery that bombarded Charlestown during the **Battle of Bunker Hill** and set that town ablaze. **Gen. John Burgoyne** used Copp's Hill as a command post during the battle and was witness to the doubly grisly sight of an entire town burning to the ground and, just beyond, an army of British regulars falling dead or wounded.

The crest of Copp's Hill was removed in 1807 for use as a millpond landfill, where **North Station** now sits, and the site of both the windmill and the British battery disappeared into the mud. For more than a decade, the hill was diminished for fill. Yet Copp's Hill endured, an irreducible element of Old Boston.

Included in its ranks are the illustrious **Mathers,** for several generations the theological principals of Boston, and **Shem Drowne** of weathervane fame. **Edmund Hartt,** builder of USS *Constitution*, rests within cannon shot of his creation; and **Robert Newman,** the sexton who is said to have signaled the Sons of Liberty with two lanterns hung in the steeple of Old North Church, is buried here, too. His tombstone rests against the iron fence along the outer western pathway of the cemetery. It is also believed that as many as 29 participants of the Boston Tea Party and at least 43 veterans of the Revolutionary War are buried in Copp's Hill.

The area near **Snowhill Street** was reserved for slave burials, although the tall black monument near the Snowhill Street fence is a memorial to **Prince Hall,** a freed slave and leader of Boston's free black community. He helped promote Boston's first school for black children when he petitioned the legislature saying that it was not right that tax money went predominately toward the education of white children. The school was officially recognized in 1812, but still had years of work ahead of it. Hall also petitioned for the abolition of slavery, protested the slave trade, and rallied when free blacks were kidnapped from Boston in 1788. He worked to establish the **African Lodge of Massachusetts,** the first black Masonic Lodge in America and served as Grand Master from 1791 to 1807. He fought tirelessly for the rights of African Americans until his death in 1807. His monument was erected by the Prince Hall Masons in 1895.

Many of Copp's Hill's old stones are gone now, having been appropriated years ago by North Enders for various uses. In fact, in the late 1800s, the superintendent of the cemetery is said to have discovered more than eighty gravestones that had been either buried in the cemetery or reused in foundations, cellars, doorsteps, and chimneys. The cemetery is still filled with many wonderful epitaphs and tombstones with quaint inscriptions. The gravestone art that you will find here is filled with symbolism. The most common symbol you will see, the **winged skull** or **death's head,** is said to date back to medieval times. Its presence in this burying ground attests to the age of the cemetery as well as the influence of the Puritan religion. You may also see cherubs or angels on the stones. These tended to be more fanciful and not as many are found in this burying ground as compared to others in Boston. Was the North End more conservative? Maybe. They seemed to lean toward the more conventional symbols such as coats of arms; there are plenty of those here. Also, if you see **willow trees** on any of the stones, this symbolizes sorrow and mourning. The intricacy of the tombstones was in direct correlation to how much money the family had.

You may also notice that many gravestones bear pockmarks. The story goes that these were caused by musket balls. The chipped stone of **Captain Daniel Malcolm,** "A True Son of Liberty . . . an enemy to Oppression," bears testimony to the pleasure of British troops in using it for target practice. Be sure to check out the plaque in the cemetery that recounts more of Capt. Malcolm's exploits.

Copp's Hill was included in the movement to transition cemeteries into places of peace. This included making walkways and planting trees, However, there were drawbacks. PHOTO BY STEPHEN W. PIETRZYK

In the 19th century there was a movement to make cemeteries into parks, peaceful places where the dead could rest and the ones left behind could pay their respects. Copp's Hill was no exception. Previous to 1833, there were few to no trees on Copp's Hill, so $50 was allocated for the purchase to beautify the area. In 1838 new walking paths were installed and gravestones moved and arranged to accommodate them. While this looks prettier and is easier for modern conveniences such as lawn mowers, most often the tombstones do not mark the actual resting places of their owners.

Copp's Hill Information

Hours: 9 a.m. to 5 p.m. daily

Admission: Free

Phone: (617) 635-4504

Wheelchair accessibility: No

Note: After leaving Copp's Hill, if you're traveling North, you'll have to make the trek across the Charlestown Bridge into Charlestown to the Charlestown Navy Yard and Bunker Hill. The route is well marked with signs and the painted red line. Once you cross into Charlestown, the route goes in two directions, one to USS *Constitution* the other to Bunker Hill. No matter which way you go, the Trail will eventually take you to both sites. We chose to present USS *Constitution* first, but the choice is yours.

USS *Constitution*

Charlestown Navy Yard

After the American Revolution, the American Navy was disbanded, and for more than a decade no warships sailed under the Stars and Stripes. By 1793, however, the Barbary pirates of North Africa were preying on US merchant vessels, demanding tribute and ransom, so on March 27, 1794, President **George Washington** signed the **Naval Armament Act** to build six ships for the defense of the nation. As part of this initiative, the 44-gun *Constitution* was built in Boston and launched on October 21, 1797.

Bostonians Who Helped

When *Constitution* was built, its copper pins came from Paul Revere's foundry, and her sails were constructed at the Old Granary, the only building in Boston large enough to accommodate the work.

She was when she was built, and has been reconstructed today to be, an awesome sight. Measuring 207 feet from stem to stern and almost 44 feet broad, this beauty displaces more than 1,900 tons of water as she moves. Her mainmast towers 210 feet into the sky, and her main topsail is the size of a regulation basketball court. Today *Constitution* is **America's Ship of State** and is the oldest commissioned warship afloat in the world. Now permanently berthed at the **Charlestown Navy Yard,** this majestic ship hosts more than half a million visitors a year and has earned the right to rest.

By July 1798 the United States had become involved in an undeclared war with France, and *Constitution* was sent on patrol in the West Indies to

A testament to true grit and service, USS *Constitution* is well worth a visit as you explore the Freedom Trail. PHOTO BY STEPHEN W. PIETRZYK

protect America's interests. In 1803 she was the flagship of a squadron sent to bring about peace with the Pasha (ruler) of Tripoli and end the persistent attacks by Tripolitan corsairs on the American merchant fleet. Under **Commodore Edward Preble,** *Constitution* led the bombardment on the city of Tripoli. In June 1805, the Pasha's emissary negotiated the draft peace treaty with the United States aboard *Constitution*.

In the meantime, the United States was trying to remain neutral in the war that had broken out between France and Great Britain, but after years of increasing British harassment of American shipping and trading, President **James Madison** declared war on Britain on June 18, 1812. While many believed that the Royal Navy was invincible, USS *Constitution* would do her part to destroy that myth. It can't be said that the victories by the American Navy had a huge impact on the outcome of the war, but it can be said that those victories certainly raised American morale. Once such victory earned this great ship her nickname of "Ironsides." On August 19, 1812, under **Captain Isaac**

Hull, USS *Constitution* engaged the British frigate HMS *Guerriere* off Nova Scotia. The captain strategically had his sailors hold fire until the ship was less than 40 yards from *Guerriere*, well within the range of the ship's carronades and long guns. Once the order was given, *Constitution* executed a full broadside on her enemy and within 35 minutes, *Gueirrere* was destroyed.

Not to Be Outgunned

While USS *Constitution* was built to carry 44 guns, she typically carried more than that, averaging between 50 and 60 guns. She was outfitted with 55 guns the day she destroyed HMS *Guerriere*, rated for 38 guns, but carrying 49; she carried 54 the day she defeated the 38-gun *Java,* which was carrying 49; and the 52 guns she was outfitted with when she fought *Cyane* (20), carrying 34, and *Levant* (18), carrying 21, helped her to bring on victory.

While Capt. Isaac Hull was strategically biding his time before ordering his men to begin unloading shots at the *Guerriere*, his ship was receiving full cannon fire. The shots were not penetrating her hull, however, but bouncing off or getting embedded. The story goes that one of *Constitution*'s crewmen happened to notice this and shouted, "Huzza! Her sides are made of iron!" thus, the ship's nickname of **"Old Ironsides"** was born.

The ship's hull, in reality, is not made of iron, but of oak, three layers of oak to be exact. The innermost and outermost layers were made of white oak, while her middle layer was America's secret ingredient. Found only along the southern US coast, live oak is five times denser than any other type of oak in the world. With this sandwiched between the two layers of white oak, "Old Ironsides" is nearly impervious to enemy fire power.

Under a new captain, **William Bainbridge,** *Constitution* continued its record of outstanding service. On December 29, 1812, off the coast of Brazil, after a spirited and terrible exchange of fire, the 38-gun frigate *Java,* carrying 49 guns, was defeated and her commander, Capt. Henry Lambert, fatally wounded. After this third American victory, the British decreed that their ships would no not do battle with the Americans unless they outnumbered them at least two to one.

What's the Scuttlebutt?

If you take a tour of USS *Constitution,* you will most likely learn the scuttlebutt about the scuttlebutt—at least I did. The word *scuttlebutt* has two definitions: It is a "butt" or a cask on a ship that contains fresh water, but it is also defined as rumor or gossip. Let me tell you what these two definitions have in common. This water butt on the ship was one of the few, if not the only place onboard where a sailor was allowed to speak freely. Very much like a modern-day office water cooler, the sailors would stop by the scuttlebutt to have some of their one-gallon-a-day ration of fresh water and swap tales and information with their fellow sailors. Although we are not sure if they exchanged truth or rumor or a combination of both, we are sure that some of the tall tales of the sea probably got their start at a ship's scuttlebutt.

Three years later, the *Constitution* again entered battle with the British when **Capt. Charles Stewart** engaged the British warships *Cyane* and *Levant* off the coast of Spain. The skillful maneuvering and deadly fire of "Old Ironsides" soon convinced Capt. Thomas Gordon Falcon of the *Cyane* that the battle was not to be won. Her colors were struck forty-five minutes after the battle started. The *Levant* fought on, but eventually disengaged for repairs. Returning to battle about two hours later, Capt. George Douglas battled with *Constitution* for over an hour before he struck the *Levant's* colors. Captain Stewart was able to bring both British frigates to the coast of Cape Verdes, where he turned over the captured British sailors. While the *Levant* was recaptured by the British shortly after that, the *Cyane* was brought home to America where she served in the US Navy until 1827.

USS *Constitution* began her Mediterranean cruise that lasted until 1828 when she returned to Boston. In 1830, a rumor circulated Boston that *Constitution* was to be destroyed. A student at Harvard, Oliver Wendell Holmes, "responded with a poem of protest. While the public outcry over the rumored threat to the ship was circulating, the Navy, on 22 September 1830, sent a directive to the Boston Navy Yard to re-build *Constitution* 'with as little delay as practicable.'" In 1835, she was once again sailing and proudly serving until being decommissioned in 1881. In 1882 she was stripped of her rigging and put to use as a Navy receiving ship in Portsmouth Navy Yard in Maine. In 1897, 100 years after her launch, **John F. Fitzgerald,** Massachusetts Congressman and maternal grandfather of President **John F. Kennedy,** spoke before Congress and presented a resolution to preserve the frigate as a memorial and have her returned to Boston for her centennial. Congress authorized minimal repairs and she was towed back, and in 1905 the historic ship was once again headed for destruction, this time as a training target for the fleet.

Americans protested, and Congress appropriated funds for external but not structural repairs. For the next 20 years, the ship remained at her pier in the Boston Navy Yard as an attraction but continued to decay. Congress had little enthusiasm for preserving *Constitution,* enacting a bill in 1925 that authorized reconstruction, but provided no funds for the work. After a public fund-raising campaign—even schoolchildren answered the call by donating their pennies—the collected sum still fell short of what was needed. Finally Congress appropriated the additional money to complete the work.

Constitution departed Boston on July 2, 1931, on one of the longest voyages of her career—her three-year, three-coast National Cruise, where huge crowds greeted her at 76 different ports over ninety stops. "Public Law 83-523" was signed by President **Dwight Eisenhower** on July 23, 1954, which directed the Navy to oversee *Constitution* and restore her, as far as practicable, to her "original appearance, but not for actual service." In 1960 she was the first historic ship given National Historic Landmark status. By 1976, the privately owned **USS *Constitution* Museum** opened and *Constitution*'s 1973–75 restoration was completed in time for the country's 200th birthday. When Queen

---

USS *Constitution* Information

Hours: 10 a.m. to 6 p.m. Tues through Sun, Apr 1 through Oct 31; 10 a.m. to 4 p.m. Thurs through Sun, Nov 1 through Mar 31 *Constitution* is open for most federal holidays, but is closed on Presidents' Day, Thanksgiving Day, Christmas Day, and New Year's Day. Tours begin at 10 a.m. and run every 30 minutes, with the last tour beginning a half hour before closing. It is suggested that you arrive at least 15 to 30 minutes before your planned tour to allow enough time to pass through security, which is strict. All regulations and restrictions that pertain to federal buildings apply here.

Admission: Free

Phone: (617) 242-5670 or 242-5671

Website: www.history.navy.mil/ussconstitution/

Wheelchair accessibility: *Constitution* is a commissioned historic warship and therefore may not be equipped to accommodate people with certain disabilities. The access ramp to the upper deck is steep, but might be manageable. *Constitution*'s Public Affairs Office asks that you contact them through their Events department (the link is on their website under "Visitor Info") to discuss a tour.

Elizabeth II and Prince Philip arrived to celebrate America's bicentennial in 1976, *Constitution* proudly offered a 21-gun salute. She was dry docked in 1992 for what would become a significant four-year restoration. It was found that through her career changes, from warship to training vessel, to receiving ship, many of the original structural elements had been changed and removed. Upon the completion of the restoration, it was determined that *Constitution* was structurally strong enough to sail. In 1997, as part of her 200th anniversary year, *Constitution* sailed under her own power for the first time in 116 years.

Today USS *Constitution* is permanently berthed at the Charlestown Navy Yard and continues to be restored and cared for by the US Navy. The mission of the **Naval History & Heritage Command**

USS *Constitution* Museum Information

The USS *Constitution* Museum is located in the Charlestown Navy Yard, but is operated by separate entities from the actual USS *Constitution*. According to its website, the museum was incorporated in 1972 as an "interpretive complement to the active duty naval vessel." It is a private, nonprofit museum that offers visitors a chance to view exhibits about the ship and the time in which she served. Everyone from children to the adults in your group will find something of interest here, including many hands-on exhibits.

Hours: 9 a.m. to 6 p.m. daily, Apr 1 through Oct 31; 10 a.m. to 5 p.m. daily, Nov 1 through Mar 31; closed Thanksgiving, Christmas, and New Year's Day

Admission: Suggested donation is $4 for adults, $2 for children, but the museum will accept any amount that is comfortable for the patron; group rates are also available for 10 or more

Phone: (617) 426-1812

Website: www.ussconstitutionmuseum.org

Wheelchair accessibility: Yes

Detachment Boston, who oversees her physical care, is to preserve and restore the ship, as far as practicable, to her War of 1812 appearance. Several times in the summer/autumn seasons, and always on the Fourth of July, "Old Ironsides" embarks on underway demonstration cruises in Boston Harbor. A testament to true grit and service, USS *Constitution* is well worth a visit as you explore the Freedom Trail.

Bunker Hill

Charlestown

The Battle

Okay, let's clear some things up right away. The name of the battle is the **Battle of Bunker Hill.** The name of the hill is **Breed's Hill.** The monument and exhibit lodge are located on Breed's Hill. It wasn't a mistake, but a strategic decision for the colonists to fortify Breed's Hill instead of **Bunker Hill.** Fighting actually took place across both of the hills, but the redoubt was built on Breed's Hill. Phew. I'm glad I got that out.

It took the courage of so many who had been pushed too far. The Crown was starting to see things unravel for her in her colonies across the ocean. Dissent was growing, men were organizing, it was time for her to move. While Parliament had responded decisively and quickly after the rebellious **Boston Tea Party** by closing the port of Boston, inserting British general **Thomas Gage** as governor, outlawing all but a few town meetings, and generally tightening its hold; it wasn't enough.

The Patriots were afoot and their numbers growing. Small bands of men across the countryside began training to provide support and the minutemen were formed. Things were heating up and no one was backing down.

The British, already in possession of Boston, realized that in order to squash the rising rebellion they needed to gain control of the surrounding areas. They started to strategize to do just that when the colonists learned of their plans and decided to beat them to it. Late in the evening of June 16, 1775, **Col. William Prescott** led 1,200 men across Bunker Hill onto Breed's Hill and built an earthen fort there, right under the noses of the British troops. Soon discovered, the colonists braced for attack.

By the early afternoon of June 17, 1775, the Battle of Bunker Hill was underway. Having set the town on fire as a distraction, 2,200 British troops set siege up the hills. They were turned back on their first two attempts and were surprised and alarmed that the colonists had defended themselves as well as they did. In fact, in later correspondence with Lord Dartmouth, Gen. Gage noted that "The rebels are not the despicable rabble too many have supposed."

Fire!

"Don't fire until you see the whites of their eyes!" was the famous order said to have been given to the Patriot soldiers as they prepared to defend Breed's Hill against the British forces. The very idea of standing your ground as this impressive, organized army made its way toward you is enough to send shivers along the spine. It is reported that this order was, in fact, an attempt by the generals to save the colonists' low supply of ammunition. They wanted every shot to count. It was not an unheard of battlefield strategy, and it must have required great courage.

On the third and final attack early in the evening, the colonists were forced to flee back over Bunker Hill. They had lost the battle, but not for lack of courage. The British officers would later refer to Breed's Hill as "a hill too dearly bought." More than 1,000 British soldiers were killed or wounded in the attack, prompting General Gage to admit that "The loss we have sustained is greater than we can bear."

The battle had been fought and hopes of reconciliation with Great Britain were diminishing, although some still hoped for such an outcome. The Revolution was on and would rage for another eight years.

A Difficult Task, an Impossible Choice

The men who joined the rebel forces during this tumultuous time in our nation's history showed great courage and strength of character. They were farmers, former slaves, store owners, people without any formal military training at all and they chose to pick up their muskets and join the forces to gain our nation's independence. Often, members of their own families would be against them, believing that the colonies belonged to Britain and that we should remain loyal. What a terrible choice to have to make between one's own family and one's own beliefs, but so many did.

One such young man and former slave, 28-year-old **Salem Poor** fought valiantly at the Battle of Bunker Hill. He showed such bravery that a petition was drafted to the General Court of the Massachusetts Bay Colony saying that Poor "behaved like an experienced officer" and that he was a "brave and gallant soldier." The document dated December, 1775, was signed by 14 officers, including William Prescott. No other such document for any other man who fought in that battle has been discovered. Poor survived as so many others had not and then went on to fight with George Washington at Valley Forge. In 1975, Poor was honored with a bicentennial postage stamp as a "gallant soldier."

The Monument

As for the famous Quincy granite monument, it almost didn't get off the ground. The first monument on the site was a wooden pillar built by King Solomon's Lodge of Masons in 1794, only 19 years after the battle, in honor of one of Boston's prominent citizens, Dr. Joseph Warren, who lost his life in the battle. However, in 1823, a group of Boston elite formed the **Bunker Hill Monument Association** and began plans for a more permanent and significant monument to commemorate the battle. Funds were raised and on June 17, 1825, the 50th anniversary of the battle, the cornerstone was laid with great fanfare. Trowel in hand, the **Marquis de Lafayette,** the nation's guest, spread the mortar. **Daniel Webster,** the rousing orator, proclaimed, "The consequences of the Battle of Bunker Hill are greater than those of any ordinary conflict."

Construction was intermittent for fifteen years, with the project experiencing multiple setbacks. By 1840, the monument was still only a little more than halfway completed when **Sarah Josepha Buell Hale**

Today, Bunker Hill monument stands at a majestic 221 feet tall atop Breed's Hill, calling to mind the courage it took to fight for our nation's birth and at what cost. PHOTO BY STEPHEN W. PIETRZYK

stepped in. Hale was the fervently patriotic daughter of a Revolutionary War officer and recent widow with the sole responsibility of five young children. She was already a published author when she became the editor for *Ladies' Magazine,* precursor of *Godey's Lady's Book,* and moved to Boston in 1827. Hale, like most Bostonians, wanted to see the memorial completed, so she, along with other prominent Bostonian women, took the unprecedented step of conducting a public fund-raising drive.

Mary Had a Little Lamb . . . Or Did She?

Sarah Hale is also credited with writing the poem we know today as **"Mary Had a Little Lamb."** First published on May 24, 1830, the poem is said to be based on the true story of Mary Sawyer who took her lamb to school with her one day. Authorship of the poem has been questioned, but most historians agree that Hale is indeed the author.

Bostonian women worked through the summer of 1840 to put together a fair and bake sale the likes of which not many had seen. It was held at the Great Hall at Quincy Market and lasted eight days. When it was done, they raised more than $30,000 (a considerable sum for the times). Two businessmen, Amos Lawrence and Judah Touro, not from Boston but still interested in helping the monument come to fruition, donated $10,000 each. These sums, plus money set aside from the previous sale of surrounding pieces of the battleground, gave the

Up, Up . . .

Visitors may climb 294 steps of the monument at Bunker Hill for a view of Boston. Be warned, however, there hasn't been an elevator here since 1844 when one was used on the outside of the monument for its construction.

association the money it needed to see the project finished. On June 17, 1843, nearly 20 years after its cornerstone had been laid, the monument was dedicated with pomp and circumstance. President John Tyler joined more than 100,000 people, including veterans from the battle and orator Daniel Webster at the dedication.

Today, the monument stands majestically 221 feet tall at the top of Breed's Hill, calling to mind the courage it took to fight for our nation's birth and at what cost.

Bunker Hill Monument Information

Hours: 9 a.m. to 5 p.m. daily with last climb at 4:30 from Sept through June; 9 a.m. to 6 p.m. with last climb at 5:30 p.m. July and Aug.

Admission: Free

Phone: (617) 242-5641

Wheelchair accessibility: Restrooms and lodge

Battle of Bunker Hill Museum Information
43 Monument Sq., Charlestown

Hours: 9 a.m. to 5 p.m. daily Sept through June, 9 a.m. to 6 p.m. July and Aug.

Admission: Free

Phone: (617) 242-7275

Wheelchair accessibility: Yes, a ramp at the entrance and an elevator inside

---

Appendix:
Where to Stay along the Freedom Trail

There are so many places to choose from in Boston if you're planning an overnight stay. We've only listed those that are in very close proximity to the Trail and we haven't even included all of them. You'll undoubtedly save money if you stay farther off the Trail and plan to drive in or take the T. If you want the convenience and ambience of the city and don't mind paying the higher rates, these will do just fine.

Ames, a Morgans Original (1 Court St.; 617-979-8120; www.morganshotelgroup.com) Named "Boston's Hippest Hotel Restaurant" by *Food and Wine Magazine,* this "modern-day tavern" is located in a building that dates back to 1893.

Boston Omni Parker Hotel (60 School St.; 617-227-8600; www.omnihotels.com/FindAHotel/BostonParkerHouse.aspx) A Boston landmark since 1855, this elegant hotel is steps from the former site of the Boston Latin School on the Freedom Trail and offers 551 luxurious guest rooms.

Boston Park Plaza Hotel & Towers (50 Park Plaza at Arlinton Street; 617-426-2000; www.bostonparkplaza.com) Located in Boston's Back Bay, this hotel offers guest rooms and suites throughout its historic property.

Club Quarters in Boston (161 Devonshire St.; 617-357-6400; www.clubquarters.com/loc_boston.php) Home to the popular Elephant & Castle Pub and Restaurant, Club Quarters in Boston offers rooms and suites just steps from the Freedom Trail.

Fifteen Beacon (15 Beacon St.; 617-670-1500; www.xvbeacon .com) In a building dating back to 1903, the XV Beacon offers 62 luxury rooms. Voted Boston's number one hotel by *Travel + Leisure* magazine.

Four Seasons Hotel Boston (200 Boylston; 617-338-4400; fourseasons.com/Boston) This Four Seasons offers 273 guest rooms, including 77 suites, with views of the Public Garden, Beacon Hill, and the Massachusetts State House.

Millennium Boston Hotel (26 North St.; 617-523-3600; www.millenniumhotels.com/millenniumboston/index.html) Overlooking Faneuil Hall and Quincy Market, this hotel is in the center of the Freedom Trail. Guest rooms and suites are available.

Nine Zero (90 Tremont St.; 617-772-5800; www.ninezero.com) Recently named one of *Travel + Leisure* magazine's "Best 500 Hotels in the World," Nine Zero is located directly across from the Granary Burying Ground.

Residence Inn Boston Harbor at Tudor Wharf (34-44 Charles River Ave.; 617-242-9000; www.marriott.com/hotels/travel/bostw-residence-inn-boston-harbor-on-tudor-wharf/) Located right on the water across the Charlestown Bridge, this Residence Inn offers 168 suites, including 12 allergy-friendly rooms. Rates include a complimentary hot breakfast buffet served daily.

Ritz-Carlton Residences, Boston Common (10 Avery St.; 617-574-7113; www.ritzcarlton.com/en/Properties/BostonCommon/Default.htm) This luxury hotel offers 193 guestrooms, including 43 suites, just a short walk from the Trail close to the Boston Common.

Taj Boston (15 Arlington St.; 617-536-5700; www.tajhotels.com/boston/) Offering 273 rooms, including 45 suites, this hotel first opened its doors in 1927. It is located near Boston's Public Garden.

Suggested Reading

As I was researching this edition of *Boston's Freedom Trail*, I relied heavily on Google Books, which is an amazing resource. There are many, many books on there for free and many more that you can purchase in electronic format. The Internet brings just about every library across the country right into your own home. Imagine being able to sit at your computer and peruse old, dusty volumes of antique books—without the dust! I often lost myself in the personal accounts of what was happening on a particular day in history as I was doing research. Here are a few that I used, but be sure to check out others that tickle your own fancies!

As a mom, I know how hard it can sometimes be to engage children and teenagers in anything educational. It just so happened that my daughter's fifth-grade class was reading *My Brother Sam Is Dead* and studying the Revolutionary War while I was writing this edition. We read a good part of this Newbery Award–winning book together and it really brought the history to life for her. I've listed it here in case you'd like to share it with your young ones. Even my six-year-old sat in on a few readings and enjoyed them.

Chambers, Robert, John Liddell Geddie, and David Patrick. *Chambers's Cyclopaedia of English Literature*. W. & R. Chambers, Limited, London and Edinburgh: 1903.

Collier, James Lincoln and Chris Collier. *My Brother Sam is Dead*. Scholastic Paperbacks: 1985.

Dearborn, Nathaniel. *Boston Notions: Being an Authentic and Concise Account of "That Village" from 1630 to 1847*. Ticknor & Company, Boston: 1848.

Drake, Samuel Adams. *A Book of New England Legends and Folklore in Prose and Poetry*. Roberts Brothers, Boston: 1888.

Drake, Samuel Adams. *Old Landmarks and Historic Personages of Boston.* James R. Osgood and Company, Boston: 1873.

Fisher, Richard Swainson. *The Progress of the United States of America.* J.H. Colton & Company, New York: 1854.

Franklin, Benjamin. *Autobiography of Benjamin Franklin.* Henry Holt and Company, New York: 1916.

Hill, Hamilton Andrews. *History of the Old South Church (Third Church).* Houghton, Mifflin and Company, Cambridge, MA: 1890.

Koren, John. *Boston, 1822–1922.* City of Boston Printing Department: 1922.

Mann, Albert W. *Walks and Talks about Historic Boston.* Mann Publishing Co., Boston: 1917.

Mantzaris, Anna. *The Freedom Trail: Boston.* Globe Pequot Press, Guilford, CT: 2010.

Martin, Tyrone G. *A Most Fortunate Ship, 2nd ed.* Naval Institute Press, Annapolis, MD: 1997.

A Memorial of the American Patriots Who Fell at the Battle of Bunker Hill. Boston City Council: 1889.

Place, Charles A. *Charles Bulfinch, Architect and Citizen.* Houghton Mifflin Company, Boston: 1925.

Quincy, Josiah. *A Municipal History of the Town and City of Boston, During Two Centuries, from September 17, 1630 to September 17, 1830.* Charles C. Little and James Brown, Boston: 1852.

Some Interesting Boston Events. State Street Trust Company, Boston: 1916.

Southworth, Susan and Michael Southworth. *The AIA Guide to Boston.* Globe Pequot Press, Guilford, CT: 2008.

Urban, Sylvanus. *The Gentleman's Guide and Historical Chronicle.* 1770.

Wilson, James Grant and John Fiske (eds.). *Appleton's Cyclopaedia of American Biography,* vol. 5. The Business Historical Society, Inc.: 1888.

Wilson, Susan. *Boston Sites and Insights: An Essential Guide to Historic Landmarks in and Around Boston.* Beacon Press, Boston, MA: 2003.

Wines, Enoch Cobb. *Trip to Boston: In a Series of Letters to the Editor of the United States Gazette.* Charles C. Little and James Brown, Boston, MA: 1838.

Index

Printed in the USA
CPSIA information can be obtained
at www.ICGtesting.com
LVHW041443011023
759827LV00044B/689